PRAISE FOR
CREATE THE LIFE YOU CRAVE

"Having led the Disney University training team at the Walt Disney corporate headquarters, consulted with top organizations around the world, and authored eight books, I know great content when I experience it. Rex Conner has captured the essence of self-development in a compact and crystal-clear formula in his new book, *Create the Life You Crave*. Developing your personal guidance system and learning to rely upon it will take anyone to new heights—both personal and professional."

–DOUG LIPP, best-selling author of *Disney U*

"*Create the Life You Crave* is a fascinating and very practical book about how to analyze and take control of your life—your career choices, your relationships with family and friends, your way of thinking. No, it doesn't dictate what you should do, but it describes how to figure out for yourself what makes sense for your life, while sharing a number of illustrative examples from people the author has known over the years. Author Rex Conner has created a truly wonderful tool."

–EILEEN MAGER, singer, writer, training consultant, and theatrical costume creator

"Rex Conner masterfully reminds us that true success in life is grounded in discovering and skillfully pursuing a personal purpose aligned with one's most passionate and personal beliefs. *Create the Life You Crave* is not only brilliant and inspiring; it's a must-read for anyone who yearns for a life of clarity, contribution, and joy."

—CLINT CAMAC, President, Leadership Development Network

"Living the life we want is difficult if we constantly consider ourselves as being subject to obstacles in our surroundings. We hear stories of how others have overcome adversity and tragedy, but we don't do the same for ourselves. If we take the principles that are mentioned in *Create the Life You Crave*, we can begin taking the steps to get where we want to be. This may be different for everyone, but the mindset and the ability to take action is necessary regardless. Rex Conner is brilliant in his approach to delivering how we can act on his message."

—LEIGH ANN MILLER, founder, Custom Leadership

"If you care deeply about your personal growth and are seeking long-term happiness in both your life and career, then put this book on your required reading list. You will learn to empower yourself and others with this no-nonsense guide to creating the life you crave. Rex Conner will teach you to use your internal guidance system to give you the boost you need to become your personal best."

—JEFFREY L. RUPP, President, Leadership Magic

"Any leader, and in fact every human, should listen to their internal guidance system—their conscience. Yet in the current world, this is neither easy nor straightforward. Rex Conner's guide on how and where to apply this guidance is easy to digest and absorb, with the potential to be crucial in many of life's situations. Rex provides something we all need to know—and do!"

–KIM NORLAND, President & CEO, Design
Success International

CREATE THE LIFE YOU CRAVE

AN UNCOMMON PATH TO A LIFE OF PURPOSE

REX CONNER

GREENLEAF
BOOK GROUP PRESS

Published by Greenleaf Book Group Press
Austin, Texas
www.gbgpress.com

Distributed by Greenleaf Book Group

For ordering information or special discounts for bulk
purchases, please contact Greenleaf Book Group at PO Box
91869, Austin, TX 78709, 512.891.6100.

Design and composition by Greenleaf Book Group
Cover design by FlashPoint Productions
Cover image: Storyblocks

Publisher's Cataloging-in-Publication data is available.

Print ISBN: 979-8-88645-034-7

eBook ISBN: 979-8-88645-035-4

To offset the number of trees consumed in the printing of our
books, Greenleaf donates a portion of the proceeds from each
printing to the Arbor Day Foundation. Greenleaf Book Group
has replaced over 50,000 trees since 2007.

Printed in the United States of America on acid-free paper

23 24 25 26 27 28   10 9 8 7 6 5 4 3 2 1

First Edition

CONTENTS

PREFACE

Political divisiveness, wars, inflation, global pandemic, and other disasters are all outside of my ability to influence. Yet they all make almost daily appearances in the news and are part of my daily life. What can an insignificant individual like me, who is not on the world stage, do about any of it? I can focus on the small influences I have to nourish relationships with my family and friends, to maintain my health, and to pursue the compelling personal purposes I have in life as I'm given to see those purposes.

The foundational message in this book is one of those purposes for me. It has occurred to me that the one activity that each person could pursue that would make the most significant impact in each life and in the world in general is to follow their conscience. It changes the life of anyone who does it, and it can change the world!

Who will this book serve?

- You, if you are facing significant crossroads decisions in your life.

- You, if all of the noise in the world leaves you feeling like you should do what you can do about it.

- You, if you feel that you should be contributing more to people or to life than you currently are, but you may not know to whom or how.

- You, if you need permission to align your life with an inner guidance that seems to be compelling you to take action that you have been avoiding.

- You, if you feel the need to develop your skills but realize the current educational options will not result in that development.

- You, if you are climbing the ladder of success but sense that it might be leaning against the wrong wall.

- You, if you are compelled to make your life something that your inner guidance will judge to be a success.

- You, if you have influence to help someone described earlier.

If any of the needs previously listed pertain to you, you will require more than just information or knowledge on the subject. You will have to apply skills. Fortunately, the most foundational of all those skills is already familiar to you. You have already developed it to some degree. You have recognized input from your internal guidance—your conscience. We all have at least some experience in following our conscience, some of us more than others. This book will reintroduce you to that foundational skill to the degree you need. It will be like reconnecting with an old friend.

As you increase your ability to recognize and follow that guidance, the realities of your life will continue to evolve and change—with you having the confidence that you are doing the best you can. You will be satisfying the judge you have always wanted to satisfy—yourself, your inner self. That will speak peace to you!

How do I know that? Clearly, I don't know you. And if I do, I don't know you well enough to know what your inner thoughts are. But we all recognize what we have in common. It's not religion. It's not spirituality. It's not a commonality of belief.

Whatever source of human nature provided it, whether you call that source God or nature or energy or love or spirit or instinct or any of the many other descriptions, we can all recognize an inner guidance system. That inner guidance resides independent of our natural desire to feed our ego, impulses, appetites, fears, or reasoning and is far superior to them all. We know that instinctively. We all have it.

Why can I write about it? For the same reasons that you could. I don't write from an academic background or from professional experience, although I have both of those credentials. It's because I try as diligently as I can to recognize how this life really works, how natural law governs everything around us except for people's decisions and actions. I fight the daily battle to stay aware of that internal guidance and to follow it. Like you, my success is limited by my humanness. But because of that awareness and those credentials, I have compelling stories to tell that illustrate many of the countless applications of following our conscience. They are stories of successes and of failures. They are stories of real life, of real people, of the drama of life.

I desperately want these stories to touch your consciousness and to lead you to a journey inward. I want you to find, deep inside of you, exactly what you want from your life and to discover how to achieve that. You won't find that through my instructions. Please consider this book's content to be simply an invitation inward to where those discoveries reside. Consider it an invitation to reconnect with an old friend who will gift to you your greatest desires. That old friend *is* the power within you!

INTRODUCTION

L ife has granted us each a wonderful gift in allowing each person the freedom to make decisions regardless of who they are, where in the world they are, or what time in history it is. Of course, no one can choose any of the results of those decisions. Those results are governed by natural laws.

Natural laws are just what they sound like: the unbreakable rules of the universe. They are a set of unavoidable forces that determine the outcomes of actions and decisions. Natural laws include physical consequences, such as falling backward if you tip your chair over, but they also involve behavior, such as the fight-or-flight response common in all animals and human nature. They govern the results of all actions except for a person's response to those actions. People choose their responses.

Gravity is the standard example of a natural law to which we all can relate. It acts the same no matter who you are, where you are, or when you are there. The results are predictable. After considering that obvious example, people generally want to see a list of natural laws. That's tough because they don't all have names and aren't all as obvious as gravity. It is much more useful to recognize the *natural results* of actions that people take.

- If you don't water plants, they dehydrate.

- If you speed in a car, your stopping distance increases.

- If animals get hungry, their effort goes into finding food.

- If the sun reflects off of objects, the glare restricts your vision.

We can call all of these natural results "blinding flashes of the obvious." Hold on to that term; it will return.

We can get the results we want in life by identifying the natural laws that govern those results, then complying with those natural laws. Yes, it is that easy.

However, there are two problems with that "easy" approach to life: We often aren't patient enough to allow natural law to work, so we seek shortcuts. We confuse human influence with the ability to bypass natural law, and we are deceived by short-term results. During that search for the shortcuts in life, our impatience, our inexperience, our short-sightedness, or our chemical impairment clouds our vision, and we think we can outmaneuver natural law. Our actions are sometimes preceded by some form of declaration such as, "Hey, hold my beer and watch this!" We hope natural law won't always apply to us. But it does.

The billions of people on this planet at any one time are wildly different in our circumstances, beliefs, desires, and decisions. There are a few commonalities among us once our basic survival needs are met. Psychologists have arranged all of these needs into general hierarchies to help us understand each other. The description that fits our purposes in this book is that we each want to fulfill our purposes in life, our own way. Navigating the demands of the governing natural laws through the maze of human influences to fulfill our purposes is what this book is about. That fact that you are reading this introduction is hopefully an indication that you would appreciate more clarity in that journey. It may also indicate that you are not yet completely satisfied with your path.

People who are unsettled in life instinctively know they are not on the journey that life is currently requiring of them. They have also discovered that they cannot depend on other people to have the insights as to what their direction should be. They often do not consciously recognize what that journey is because the noise of life has drowned out their internal guidance that gives them that clear insight. There is so much noise to navigate as we each try to validate that we are doing what we should be doing in this life.

So, we search. We all search at different times in our lives. Different people search through different avenues, trying to find answers. Some of the most common pathways we try to find answers through are these:

- Science

- Religion

- Education

- Psychology

- Medicine

- Culture

- Energy Modalities

- Philosophy

Each of those is ultimately one way to attempt to understand and apply natural law, which governs all the results of our actions in this life. The problem is that no single one of those avenues contains *all* the answers for any individual. People who devote their entire lives to only one of those pursuits will acknowledge that you cannot find all of life's answers in a single field of study or even through a combination. The scientist must rely on hypotheses, models, and various—sometimes inconclusive—experiments. Even the religious can't offer definite answers to all of life's questions, and so our search continues.

Each of the fields of study on that list is a way we can relate to life, but each stops short of a complete understanding of how life works for us *personally*. As a result, when our quest for answers stops short in some way or another, we are forced to rely on our own limited experience and understanding, which give us the inconsistent results we encounter in life.

A shorter path to finding our individual journey is for us to identify, follow, and observe natural laws and consequences as we encounter them. *Awareness* of the natural laws and their conse-quences in our daily lives is where our personal journey lies.

But there *is* a sequence to be followed. We'll get consistent results in our lives *when we have the sequence right.* The sequence we need is to first determine *what* to do in life before trying to figure out *how* to do it.

Actually, the way successful businesses are run is a good model for life. In business, as in other pursuits, leaders first determine what they want to achieve. *Then*, they determine the path the business is to follow to achieve the goal. Next, managers determine how to move down that path. If the leaders haven't determined the path to follow, and the managers spend time and resources without having clear direction, time and resources can be wasted.

With so much noise and so many choices for our personal jour-ney, isn't it bizarre that we all end up wanting basically the same result out of this life? The journey is a wildly different one for each of us, but in the final analysis, most of us want our life to have had some meaning, purpose, or fulfillment. We want to have mattered or to have made a significant difference. And in the final analysis, only one voice matters as the judge.

Before the final analysis, we need to be settled that what we are doing with our life is the right journey for right now. The journey is all that matters. That same voice that judges the final analysis is the only one that settles our current concern. Until we have that set-tling judgment, we are in grave danger . . . the danger that haunts those with regrets.

I hope to reintroduce you to that voice, as if to reintroduce you to an old friend. Please allow this exercise to make that introduction.

Exercise

Access your conscience and ask it, "What three practices should I either start or stop to have the greatest positive impact in my life?" What does your conscience tell you?

Don't continue until you've completed the exercise and have determined the three practices.

The point of this exercise is *NOT* for you to share the result with anyone. The point *IS* for you to realize that it probably didn't take long at all for your conscience to point out the three practices to you. For most people, the exercise takes less than three minutes.

It happens so quickly because you are already connected to your conscience, the all-important guidance system within you. You constantly choose the degree to which you follow it, but you are already connected. Your conscience, in turn, is connected to the natural laws and consequences that govern all of life's experiences. Your internal guidance system *is* your conscience . . . and it is *really* good!

Why are we so influenced by the noise of the world? Why do we so easily follow the influence of the media, politicians, society, or other people? Why are we even more prone to follow our own limited experience, reasoning, ego, and impulses when we have constant, direct access to the power that governs all of life's experiences?

Common Sense Isn't Very Common

Receiving guidance from the right source is the first step in a new way to master your many important decisions in life. If you currently make important and even daily decisions in your life by using your reasoning to think through the options, or by asking other people in your life for their input, this book is an invitation to consider a new way. The new way is your uncommon sense.

Common sense is that voice inside every one of us that tells us when we should and should not do certain things. It is our instinct. It is our conscience. It is our internal guidance system. It has many other names. In short, it is our personal connection with natural law, natural consequences, and with the guidance of what we should be doing with our lives. It is the judge that matters most to us!

We can observe and predict the outcome of many of the situations we encounter in life with relative confidence. When several people observe the same situation and all predict the same outcome, we call that common sense.

What we are really doing in that situation is observing natural laws and predicting the consequences of the actions taking place. While we don't always know the time frame, we know that natural law will win in the long run.

For example, when a person jumps off a tall building to prove they can fly without a flying contraption, we predict an ugly ending. Even when we hear the person about halfway down shouting out, "See, I told you I could fly!" or "So far, so good!" our common sense knows the inevitable outcome.

Uncommon sense, on the other hand, is simply having the awareness and courage to follow your common sense. Consider this: the most repeated phrase about common sense is some version of "Common sense isn't very common!" Why is that such a widely accepted observation of common sense?

This book does not have the answer for that question. But it does recognize the reality of many of us ignoring our internal guidance, or our common sense, much of the time. Since taking the time to access our common sense, and then to follow it, is uncommon, in this book we are calling it our uncommon sense.

When you assess the value of your contributions to life, at any point in your life, your standard of judgment will be how often and how thoroughly you followed your uncommon sense. When you are aware of that uncommon sense, your judgment of yourself will be the only one that matters. You will consider your life to be a success, or not, by the degree to which you follow your internal guidance.

CHAPTER 1

YOUR COMPELLING PERSONAL PURPOSES

Musicians must make music, artists must paint, poets must write if they are ultimately to be at peace with themselves. What humans can be, they must be.

—ABRAHAM Maslow

I knew as a child that I was going to be a US Air Force fighter pilot. My dad was a fighter pilot, and even though he died when I was nine, I figured it was in my blood—it was just supposed to be. That gave me motivation to do well in school when I might have otherwise been distracted. That is why I qualified for an ROTC scholarship and went to college. I did well in college in order to fulfill this dream. Yes, I was passionate about it.

Just before college graduation, I took my first flight physical to complete my qualifications. I was confident, healthy, and even cocky.

I failed the color vision test. I wasn't *completely* color-blind, but I could not see most of the numbers hidden in the different colored dots of the test. I was told this disqualified me as a pilot.

That was it—my quest was over. Dumbfounded, I asked the attending technician if there was any other way. He said there was an alternative test they could give, but it usually got the same results. I was directed to a dark room to sit alone for ten minutes while my eyes adjusted, and then they would show me colored lights that I would have to identify for the alternative test.

Those ten minutes alone, as I waited for the alternative test to begin, were the proverbial "come to Jesus" moments for me. For the first time, I searched past my ego and passion to ask my uncommon sense if being a pilot was what I was supposed to be doing with my life. In the quiet darkness, an answer came to me. I became aware that my purpose was not my occupation. No, my purpose was *who* I was and *who* I was becoming. Occupations, accomplishments, and life experiences would come and go, but I was to have purposes throughout my life, regardless of my circumstances. I would find my compelling purposes along the way.

That uncommon sense instruction to me went on to establish that, since being a pilot wouldn't disqualify me from those larger life purposes, I could experience being a pilot for a time without missing out on my larger goals. I did not understand just what that meant at the time, but it caused me to stay aware of what life was offering to me along the way. I was confident that I would find more meaningful purposes for me.

I passed the alternative color vision test and had a wonderful experience of fulfilling that dream of flying for the Air Force for the next eight years. By the time my service was over, I had developed a new passion. I was able to leave flying without regret and without feeling unfulfilled. I have since then been able to pursue teaching natural law, which hadn't been any part of my original plan, but which grew into a passion that, I believe, will remain with me as long as I have breath and capacity.

The transition from the passion that my ego had chosen—to be a pilot—to the path validated by my uncommon sense certainly wasn't what I envisioned before then. Other people with experience in realizing their lifetime passions have confirmed that *their* passions grew out of the experiences that life offered to them along the way. They hadn't planned them either.

I had learned that flying wasn't my life's purpose after all, but was simply one step along life's path. Purpose is who we are, not what we do. And purpose happens every day.

When you are living the life that your uncommon sense validates and you make your daily choices in order to live that life, you are living deliberately. The opposite of living deliberately is drifting or living the life someone else expects of you or the life your circumstances have shaped for you without you validating them with your uncommon sense. That is not living!

Life's Purposes Happen Daily

Your life's purposes happen daily. That's not a typo. It's purposes—plural.

We use the descriptions "life purpose" or "destiny," but that can mislead some people into thinking about one great, crowning achievement. You may or may not have one large, culminating purpose or destiny in your life for which you are known and remembered.

That's wonderful if you do! You also have purposes every day. They are contributions, big and small, that only you are in a position to make. The process of life leads you to become aware of your purposes. This awareness does not come from other people. It comes from your internal guidance system—your uncommon sense. Your purposes are more of a result of who you are than what you do.

The Source of Your Purpose

You choose your purposes in life. I know some of you readers are religious and will adamantly claim that God gives you your purpose, but please hear (read) me out on this!

If your life were to end at this instant (heaven forbid!), your purposes would be defined by who you have become up until this moment. You are the result of the combined decisions you have made leading up to this moment. In that case, regardless of what anyone else claims your purposes should have been, you have become and contributed whatever you chose to become and contribute up until now.

If you believe you are not on the path to whatever you believe your purposes to be, there is only one person responsible for putting you on that path.

For this topic to impact you, think of a person you know personally who regrets the life they have lived. Then, as you read on, make sure you can avoid being like that person.

In the meantime, let's explore the four most probable types of a person you could be when it comes to making decisions and thus your purposes in life:

- People who react only to their circumstances, impulses, ego, fears, and appetites in life make decisions that result in their purposes being self-preservation and self-gratification.

- People who allow others to do their thinking for them make decisions based on what other people, institutions, or society expects of them.

- People who think independently and use their own reasoning or passions without guidance from their uncommon sense have goals and visions of purposes to pursue.

- People who allow their uncommon sense to validate their goals and visions ensure that as they climb the ladder of success, the ladder they are climbing is the correct one. They live life deliberately and without regrets!

Purpose—Mission—Passion

There is no shortage of literature, podcasts, TED Talks, lectures, and other sources of guidance on the role of your life's purpose, life mission, or on pursuing your passions. In fact, there is so *much* that it sometimes becomes confusing. For the purposes of this book, let's clarify how we are using these terms.

We will use the terms "life purpose" and "life mission" as though they were the same. Each describes what you are doing with your life. For the phrase "pursuing your passion" to have the same meaning, you must distinguish between the two different types of passions, explained as follows.

The first type of passion is part of the human condition, the passions that grow out of our desires, appetites, impulses, and ego. These passions can be wonderful, but they want to control us. Unchecked, these passions give pleasure, then become habits, and eventually enslave us. They battle against the other type of passion because they want to be the only driving force.

The other source of passion grows out of our natural desire to contribute to life. We almost always express this passion in our service to others, or in taking care of ourselves so we can be of service to others. We recognize it when we realize that we have "gifts" or abilities that allow us to contribute in an extra ordinary— extraordinary—way. These gifts often don't start out as passions but as requirements that life or circumstances force upon us.

For example, my passion to teach natural law wasn't my original one. Most of the US' Founding Fathers didn't start out with a passion for establishing a new country. One of the traits they had in common was a passion for individual freedom, which led to the rest. You can find countless examples of meaningful passions growing along the journey. These examples demonstrate people living with full purpose of heart!

The reality is, your purposes in life don't usually start out as your passions. Your purposes in life *become* your passions! In this book, these passions are the same as your compelling personal purposes and your life mission.

Purpose Is Not as Much What You *Do* as It Is Who You *Are*

Many people don't relate to having purpose in life because they view it as just another role they should have (e.g., teacher, plumber, doctor, family member, athlete, artist), or accomplishments they should be pursuing (writing a book, becoming a celebrity, finding a cure for the common cold). But the reality is that roles and accomplishments come and go in life, while your purpose is who you are and who you are becoming as a person every day of your life. Throughout your life you will have several roles and many accomplishments, and each one will contribute to your life purpose.

That purpose is defined daily and evolves throughout your life. It enables you to choose the roles you'll play and the accomplishments you'll work toward. It guides your efforts, analyzes your results, and enables you to further develop your purpose as life goes on. Yes, you may have major accomplishments or play a variety of roles, but your life and its purpose will develop before, during, and after those accomplishments and those roles.

Attaining public recognition for an artistic, heroic, or outstanding achievement of some sort is admirable. But it does not replace that person's ability and innate necessity to continue with accomplishments or their need to set and achieve goals. It simply underscores that they—and we—live an entire life with the opportunity to contribute.

A retirement community is a place that shines light on the importance of not confusing a role with a purpose. So many people work toward retirement but don't find activities that bring them meaning after the identity of their profession or daily family responsibilities are gone. These people search for activities to fill the time, while feeling irrelevant or empty inside.

What's Best for the Child

Being aware of your purpose becomes your anchor in the storm and your standard for mastering life's transitions, as the following story illustrates.

Kailey wasn't normally a party girl—but she was going to be this night. She had received enough grief from her roommates about being a twenty-year-old "goody-goody," and she hadn't made friends as easily in her new location as she had in the past. So, in these new surroundings, two thousand miles away from home, family, and friends, she was going to fit in and enjoy the party—all of it—whatever it brought.

A few weeks later, she realized she needed to act on a hunch that came to her while talking to her best friend by phone. She decided to take a pregnancy test. As soon as she saw those two blue lines indicating a positive test, her uncommon sense communicated clearly to her. Her world immediately changed when she realized "I'm a mom now. Nothing else matters. I have to do what is best for this baby."

As her head and emotions caught up to the new reality, she knew she had never done anything this difficult before, but that didn't matter. She knew she would receive both judgment and advice from people she loved. She would have to make a life decision about keeping the baby or not. The fear, ego, self-interests, reasoning, and emotions all came at once, questioning what her uncommon sense had already established. But she held firm to the guidance she had received through her uncommon sense. She now had a compelling personal purpose: "I'm a mom. I have to do what is best for this baby."

She was right. She had never done anything this difficult in her life. As each challenge to her compelling personal purpose of being a mom reared its head, she worked through it. She never doubted her purpose. Her energy went into figuring out how to accomplish what she knew she had to.

The baby's father opted out of the picture. She let everyone, including her parents, share their opinions and give their advice. She thanked them all, then made her own decision, which was contrary to much of the advice she had received. She decided to keep the baby. Her reasoning aligned completely with her purpose. She would do what was best for the child from her own insights.

She explained, "If I give the baby up for adoption, at some point in life this person [not yet knowing the gender] will want to meet his/her mom and will have questions. When it's apparent that I went on with my life, later married and had other children, the natural question will be, 'Why didn't you just keep me?' I never want this child to feel unwanted, unimportant, or like she/he was an inconvenience or a mistake."

That wasn't the easy path for Kailey, but it was the best for the *baby*—that important *other* person involved. It might not be the path that others should take, but Kailey knew it was hers. How did she know?

Kailey knew she had a conscience but rarely made following it a conscious effort. When she purposely listened to it at this critical crossroads in her life, she knew what she had to do. She did not know *how*, but she knew *what*.

In the seven years to date following that initial establishment of her purpose, Kailey is continuing the path. She has married, and she has had a second child. The family of four is working hard to establish a good life. Kailey holds to her compelling personal purpose of doing what is best for her family.

Making those tough life transitions, then handling the difficult road afterward is what life is about. It's about your next crossroads decision, not your past decisions. It's about what you will create from this point, whether you are sixteen or sixty years old. This practice of living deliberately may not be the common or the popular approach to living life, but it is the way that you will master life's transitions!

Stick to the Path

When you allow your uncommon sense to identify the path you should be walking and you follow it, you feel the peace and contentment we all yearn for during our lives. When you knowingly choose to not follow that path, you do not enjoy that peace. You are in conflict with yourself, and your path to finding that peace becomes long, winding, and arduous. When you don't yet recognize that path, you are unsettled and searching for it.

One of the great moments in life is the confirmation from your own internal guidance system that, given the realities in your lifetime today, you are doing the best you can. You then know that you are fulfilling your purposes in life.

Your uncommon sense never goes away. It will always, realistically, lead you to choose the best path to peace and contentment available to you. When you choose to ignore its guidance, the path back to peace is still there. People commonly try to ignore it, to medicate it, to outwork it, or to cover it with the self-indulgence of their choices. Those people must live with the consequences. As John Wayne is credited with saying, "Life's tough, but it's tougher when you're stupid." All of us spend some part of our lives off of that path. In times of wisdom, we return to it the best we can.

Recognizing Your Purposes

A story of the Buddha applies here. It is said that, soon after his enlightenment, the Buddha passed a man on the road who was struck by the Buddha's extraordinary radiance and peaceful presence. The man stopped and asked, "My friend, what are you? Are you a celestial being or a god?"

"No," said the Buddha.

"Well, then, are you some kind of magician or wizard?"

Again, the Buddha answered, "No."

"Are you a man?"

"No."

"Well, my friend, then what are you?"

The Buddha replied, "I am awake."

You don't have to embrace religion to become awake and to live life deliberately. You don't have to be as advanced as the Buddha to follow your uncommon sense. You must simply wake up and be aware.

I regularly speak with a few people in my life I consider my "mastermind" group. They have wisdom beyond their years, and most of them have years beyond mine. I asked one of the sages if he thought we needed quiet times in our lives to hear our uncommon sense. His response was priceless.

"I dunno . . . Quiet time works about 50/50 for me. Sometimes I hear my conscience. Sometimes I fall asleep and take a nap!"

He went on to share that the key is to have awareness, rather than worrying about listening. Fortunately, recognizing and following your uncommon sense doesn't require quiet or stillness. It can be done even in the hectic environment of daily life.

As a result of his insight, I started practicing awareness during spin class. In spin class you are peddling on a stationary bike in the dark with distractions all around you and music playing loudly. An instructor is shouting out instructions to you over the loud music. That's where I try to stay aware of what my uncommon sense would direct me to do with the next few hours of my life. Sure enough, you don't need peace and quiet to stay aware of guidance from your uncommon sense.

When you are aware, you know when a course of action is right. The results of your actions validate your common sense. You can learn about the guidance from your uncommon sense by observing your own life or by observing the lives or teaching of others.

Since the key to choosing the best path is about awareness, start by evaluating the many times in your own life when you made decisions, good or bad, and learned from the consequences of those decisions. When you recognize the times you went against your own judgment, gut, or instinct (your uncommon sense) and regretted it, you will realize how to be aware.

Even during the routine events of the day, you'll know when you are or are not following your uncommon sense. Think of the last time you did not follow it. You probably don't have to think back far. For example, when was the last time you did the following:

- Ate or drank something you shouldn't have

- Didn't follow a traffic law you should have

- Mistreated someone who didn't deserve it

- Did something wrong, then tried to cover it up

How did you feel about those decisions?

Or, on the positive side, when was the last time you consciously chose the right direction in one of those decisions? How did you feel *then*?

Your examples probably came to mind easily. That is how you learn to follow your uncommon sense. You consciously recognize when you are receiving that guidance and pay attention to the consequences of the decisions you make to follow it or to ignore it. Yes, it's that simple!

Your awareness of your purposes may come as a sudden blinding flash of the obvious, as in the case of Kailey understanding the guidance "I have to do what is best for this baby." Or your awareness may come to you along the way, as in my case of realizing that I should be teaching natural law. In either case, your uncommon sense is leading you to your compelling personal purposes. As you recognize your internal guidance more and more often, your confidence in following it grows.

The Sequence Is All Important

Whenever we make a decision, especially the big decisions about life's transitions, there is a sequence to follow. We need to first determine the path we should take, and then figure out how to conduct the journey on that path. Our first resource to access in determining the path is our uncommon sense. Don't wait to access your internal guidance until after you have clouded its message with reasoning and input from other people.

WARNING:

Pursuing your passions can be a fatal error when you get the sequencing wrong!

For example, notice in the story of pregnant twenty-year-old Kailey that she listened to her uncommon sense tell her right away *what* to do—to make her decision based on what was best for this baby. What might have happened had she not made her decision first? What effect might the onslaught of well-meaning advice from so many people have had on her? How about the effect of her own reasoning, her own ego, her fears, or her own impulse of wanting the easy way out?

So, is it wrong to listen to our reasoning and to get guidance from others? No—as long as we keep the steps in the right sequence. When we need to make a decision of what to do, in which direction to go, our decision needs to be guided by our uncommon sense. Then we allow our head or reasoning to catch up so we can make some sense of it and figure out how to proceed down that path.

Thomas Carlyle said it like this: "It is the heart always that sees before the head can see."

If we start by determining the destination with reasoning, fear, ego, or with impulses or appetites, we can travel a long time in the wrong direction, even a lifetime! Our uncommon sense is the initial resource for leading our life and is the single most important component of recognizing our life's purposes.

Use Your Gifts

You have gifts in life for use in fulfilling your purposes. Awareness and development of your gifts will naturally lead you to purposes. So, how do you recognize those gifts?

"The fish will be the last to discover water."[1] Like the fish discovering water, it's difficult for you to recognize your gifts that constantly surround and are a part of you. When you are gifted in an area of life and can perform effortlessly, you tend to think that everyone else can perform similarly. It isn't until you realize that others cannot do what you can do naturally that you notice that you are gifted in that area. Here is my example.

During Air Force pilot training, I was working hard to develop the many required skills. I was getting pretty good performance evaluations. One day, I overheard a couple of the instructor pilots talking about one of the student pilots who was truly gifted and excelling far beyond the others. I hoped they were talking about me. They weren't!

It wasn't until I flew with a truly gifted pilot that I realized the difference. I could work hard to develop skills, but I would never have the abilities of those for whom flying was second nature because of their gifts. When those people work hard to further

---

1   "We Don't Know Who Discovered Water, but We Know It Wasn't a Fish," Quote Investigator, accessed June 11, 2022, https://quoteinvestigator.com/tag/james-c-coleman/.

their skills, they achieve a realm of performance that we mere mortals can only admire. This is common in the world of athletics and the performing arts. The fact that I was a good but not a gifted pilot was another indication to me that flying wasn't my purpose, even though it was a passion.

You have gifts. The way the natural laws of life work is that your gifts are related to your purposes in life. That is not to say that if playing a musical instrument comes easily to you that you should be a musician as a profession. But a gifted musician can apply their skills in many different ways to fulfill numerous purposes that life presents them.

Your gifts may not be performance based. I have a family member who doesn't feel gifted because others have gifts that make them influencers on TikTok. That family member is incredibly gifted in organizing on a professional level and is constantly acknowledged as an administrative marvel. Other people have gifts of listening, providing compassionate service, making others feel acknowledged, and other people-oriented skills that aren't featured in talent shows.

Exercise

It will be beneficial for you to acknowledge some of your gifts, right now, right here in private. No one else needs to know, so you don't have to be modest. Take the time to record here, or somewhere else that works for you, at least three of the gifts you have in life. If you honestly don't recognize at least three of your gifts, ask for the input of someone in your life who knows you well.

_____

_____

_____

_____

Consider now how these gifts might be used for various purposes in your life.

Insights to Purposes from Those Who Know

The Congressional Medal of Honor is the highest military recognition that can be awarded. Most honorees don't live to receive it. This story of William Crawford is a happy exception that illustrates that there are many purposes in life.

Perhaps it was the way he carried himself in an unassuming and humble manner, but day after day, hundreds of Air Force Academy cadets would pass this janitor in the hall oblivious to the greatness that was among them.

In the mid-1970s, William Crawford might spend one day sweeping the halls and another cleaning the bathrooms, but it was a day approximately 30 years prior that would create for him a special place in the history of war. In 1943 in Italy, the only thing Private William Crawford was cleaning out was German machine gun nests and bunkers.

Under heavy fire and at great risk to himself, his gallantry was so audacious that it earned him the Medal of Honor and the respect of any man who witnessed his actions.

The cadets would report that the shy janitor they only knew as Mr. Crawford simply blended into the background as he did his job without much fanfare. However, when one of the cadets began reading a book detailing the Allied advance through Italy he came upon the story of a Medal of Honor recipient named William Crawford.

The cadet made the connection and exclaimed to his roommate, "Holy cow, you're not going to believe this, but I think our janitor is a Medal of Honor [recipient]." The next day, the cadet took the book to Crawford and simply asked if this was him.

Perhaps weighing whether it was worth it to expose his gallantry, Crawford stared at the book for a while then simply said, "That was a long time ago and one day in my life."[2]

---

2   Adapted from: Col. Bill Parker U.S. Marines (ret.), "The Story of Private William Crawford," BlowingRocket.com, November 11, 2016, https://www.wataugademocrat.com/blowingrocket/the-story-of-private-william-crawford/article_71a53fb6-92da-5be7-baf4-4f9ab3f7530d.html.

We don't know how William Crawford would have assessed the thousands of days of his life surrounding that moment of extraordinary valor. But *that's* the point! Even though we might assess his life as being extraordinary, based on his recognized valor, it was his internal guidance—his uncommon sense—that was, to him, the only valid judge of his life, of the several contributions he made during his life, and of that one day that put him in the history books. He knew that day in battle didn't define his entire life's contributions.

When a person attains public recognition or has an outstanding achievement, we tend to think of that as their life's purpose. But that's dangerous for any of us because there is a lot of life to live outside of that spotlight that is not tied to that recognition or achievement.

Another Congressional Medal of Honor recipient teaches that message to us directly. Bernard F. Fisher was the first aviator to receive the nation's highest military honor during the Vietnam War.

Major Fisher led a small squadron of planes that had been sent to help Special Forces commandos who were under attack that day at an isolated camp near the South Vietnam-Laos border, according to the Air Force. While the squadron was strafing North Vietnamese positions, a shell destroyed the engine of one plane, forcing the pilot to crash-land.

Major Fisher saw the plane skid and burst into flames and the pilot, Major Dafford "Jump" Myers, leap from the wreckage and disappear into the underbrush. Major Fisher radioed for a helicopter, then decided there was not enough time, telling radio controllers he would get Major Myers himself.

Landing for the rescue, Major Fisher overshot the runway, damaging the tail section of his plane. He had just turned the plane around to begin his search when Major Myers sprinted into view. Major Fisher pulled him into the cockpit headfirst, and they took off. "We didn't even strap in," he said.

He was often asked why he took the risk, landing on an airstrip littered with debris and surrounded by hills bristling with guns. He barely knew Major Myers; they were from different units and had met on only two or three occasions. He had the same answer nearly every time: a comrade in arms was about to be killed, and he believed he could save him.

"It's important that you respond to your feelings when the time comes for it," he often said when talking about the experience.[3]

Being part of an organization that was honored to carry the name of then retired Colonel Bernard F. Fisher, I got to meet him and hear him speak on several occasions. The heroics that earned him the Medal of Honor took place in less than an hour during one day of his life. However, he described the guidance that led him to take action on that fateful day as his constant companion. While humbly acknowledging his status as an imperfect human, Colonel Fisher lived his daily life striving to follow that same guidance—what this book is calling his uncommon sense. It helped him recognize the many purposes he should pursue both before and after the fateful day.

The critical part of recognizing your purposes is to allow your uncommon sense to be your guide.

You probably personally know people who spent a significant portion of their lives climbing the ladder of success, only to then

---

3 I heard this story personally from Colonel Bernard F. Fisher on a number of occasions, most recently in October 1979.

discover that the ladder was leaning against the wrong wall! That wasn't where they truly wanted to be. Or maybe they lost what they wanted along the way . . . maybe key relationships. They did not allow their uncommon sense to be their guide.

Well, this chapter had a lot to say about a subject that, ultimately, only you can discover. This summary describes what's in store for you, and the QR code that follows leads you to a beautiful song that characterizes the reward for your efforts:

 Your compelling personal purposes are found by following your uncommon sense every day . . . and the results will be GLORIOUS!

Exercise

Do you already have some insights as to what your daily purposes are and where they will lead in your life? Record at least two of those purposes, and project where they might lead you:

_____

_____

_____

_____

_____

CHAPTER 2

YOUR DAILY GUIDANCE

If you have a compass, you won't get lost at sea. If you
have a conscience, you won't get lost in life.

—Matshona Dhliwayo

Full purpose of heart can drive you every day. Your purposes may change in the many circumstances in which you find yourself in life. They may change daily. It's why you get up in the morning. It's the slow grind, which is exemplified by Isaiah Thomas's story.

Mr. Irrelevant is the description given every season to the last player selected for a professional basketball team in the NBA. Mr. Irrelevant in 2011 was five-foot-nine-inch point guard Isaiah Thomas. It wasn't enough for Isaiah to achieve the impossible of being in the NBA at five feet nine. No, Isaiah had to excel. By the end of the 2017 season, he was voted fifth Most Valuable Player in the entire league of superstars and was anticipating signing a nine-figure contract. NINE figures! It was a meteoric rise by any measure. Isaiah also has a personality, humility, and an attitude that makes him a fan favorite. He was in the well-deserved limelight, on top of the world.

The closing of that 2017 season came with an injury. That injury forced him to sign for "only" low seven figures and kept him out of most of the next season and much of the following two seasons as he worked to repair the injury and return to his former playing abilities. Can you imagine going from such a public, shining spotlight that comes with such fame to the lonely, unobserved weight room and gym day after day, hour after hour, for years, not knowing your future? Early in that process, Isaiah started calling it the "slow grind." During the slow grind, which continues even into 2022, Isaiah is working as hard to return to the NBA as he did to get there, even though there are no guarantees.

The slow grind is what gets him out of bed every day to work out when he would rather be enjoying the game, the spotlight, and the riches that come with a life he previously experienced. It's what fuels a daily routine that has little glamour and a lot of hard, painful work. But it's also what provides hope and purpose that his daily effort, which is the best he can do in his present situation, will bring him success. It's what his heart pushes him to do. It is his current purpose. It's currently his full purpose of heart.

Your life may not be as glamorous as Isaiah's has been. You may not have the opportunity for fame and glory that very few have. But you have purposes every day, and you can contribute every day. Each daily grind is your opportunity to have the satisfaction of realizing, "Given my current situation in life, I am doing the best I can." And even when your future is uncertain, the realization that comes from your daily grind can bring you the peace and satisfaction that you truly want out of this life. Your life's work evolves on a daily basis. Your life's purpose is a sum total of daily purposes, not a snapshot of a single accomplishment.

Here are a few noncelebrity examples of daily purposes to show that everyone has them:

> Melissa is the mom of four boys. The oldest is five, followed by three-year-old twins, and a one-year-old—not all of them planned. Melissa feels her full-time purposes are wrapped around her marriage and her children. She doesn't apologize for missing out on friends, a job, many family and social events, and a lot of sleep. No one around her has heard her complain even once. It's a daily grind driven by compelling personal purposes.

> Lisa is a nurse practitioner who specializes in women's health. Early in her practice, she discovered that a medical condition that affects more than 5 percent of women was commonly misunderstood in the medical community and mistreated. The long-term effects lead to heart conditions and diabetes. Her study of how to help her patients was unrelenting. She became a recognized expert on the subject, writing books both for medical practitioners and for patients with the condition. What started as an

interest in helping some patients became a compelling personal purpose.

Jennifer feels trapped by the "golden handcuffs" in her career with a popular tech company. However, she is driven by her desire to develop the people who work for her and by her family's well-being. Her purposes are serving people. The job simply supports her habit.

Those are just a few examples of people living everyday lives driven by purposes. Each of those purposes will change with time and circumstances. The sum total of those contributions over a lifetime brings the satisfaction of full purpose of heart.

Habits Determine Destiny

We make thousands of decisions every day. Some studies suggest the number of daily decisions is as high as thirty-five thousand. We obviously can't make that many decisions consciously. By necessity, the majority of our decisions are made through the habits we have developed.

You can probably think of a few dozen habits that you developed consciously, like driving a car. But what about the many dozens of habits that you developed unconsciously, without putting much thought into them? Most habits are not developed consciously, but subconsciously. What generally stimulates those habits? Appetites, impulses, ego, meeting other people's expectations, previous experiences, or rationalizing are common stimulants. The point is that we have not developed many habits that are aligned with our compelling personal purposes once we recognize what they are. In many cases our habits work against those purposes.

My eating habits, for example, have been horrible most of my life. I didn't consciously *decide* to eat horribly; I just mindlessly ate what I wanted when I wanted and avoided foods I didn't like. My impulses and attitudes were far more significant in developing those eating habits than deliberate decision-making was. When I decided in ninth grade that I should be a football player, the aforementioned eating habits had resulted in me being too slow to play a skill position and too flabby to play a power position. The combination of natural law preventing my sudden commitment to healthy habits to get me in shape in time for the ninth-grade season, and my lack of long-term motivation for a football career ensured that it would not become a compelling personal purpose for me.

Fortunately, we are surrounded by plenty of positive examples of people who have developed good habits so we can all benefit from their performances. Whether it's athletes, musicians, professionals who paid the price of disciplined study and practice, or even family members who show us an example of building habits to break a destructive trait, we have plenty of evidence of the value of positive-habit-building to align with natural laws in each of our lives.

Since natural law governs the consequences or outcomes of *all* our decisions, we can easily see why we are where we are in life (both the good and the bad). We are the sum total of all the decisions we have made within the realities of our life. Thus, our life is largely the sum total of our habits.

There is no shortage of literature on developing or changing habits, so that is not the purpose of this book. The encouragement here is for you to decide which of many habits you will decide to develop or change to assist you in achieving your compelling personal purposes. Here is one suggestion:

Will you develop this most important habit of your life?

You probably already know from experience that changing or developing a habit is tough. It's even tougher when you are attempting to deny your appetites, impulses, and ego in favor of being disciplined. What would cause you to develop the difficult habit of accessing your conscience every time you face a decision of what to do with your time?

This is probably a new concept for you. It is not natural for most people. You will find little information, justification, and instruction on the topic. It simply isn't the road most traveled. Here is Scottee's insight that will probably be close to your own thoughts on the subject:

> You can find people talking or writing about building good habits, and about the benefits of following your conscience, and about using your time effectively. You never hear or read about doing all three of those practices together.
>
> When you hear of doing all three for the first time, it just seems like common sense, so the impact may not be too great. Well, if common sense is uncommon, this is probably the best example of that!

Of course, we should establish the habit of following our conscience to determine how to use our time—all of our time. And of course that would positively impact every aspect of our lives. Why haven't I heard that or thought of that before? I don't know. It seems like a blinding flash of the obvious.

Will I do it? I don't know. I just have to stay conscious of what my future self would want. Your future self should be someone you care about the most. You should be willing to do anything for that someone. Changing in such a way that I honestly allow my conscience to guide me so consistently would mean that I care enough about my future self to put in that type of tremendous effort.[4]

You might not know if you will do it either. In order to establish that habit, you would have to believe that it would positively impact your life. If you believe that, why *wouldn't* you do it?

After all, isn't that the process of life? When our desires, appetites, and passions conflict with natural laws, don't we do what we want anyway until life beats us into submission? Isn't it a common sequence to discover that what we truly want in the long run comes from doing what our conscience directs? The wise people among us are those who observe the mistakes of others and don't repeat those mistakes in their own lives.

---

4   Scott Conner, personal conversation with author, February 2022.

Exercise

Think about three of your own habits, three things you do every day and that you may not think much about. List them here:

_____

_____

_____

_____

_____

Now, evaluate each of those habits. Do they lead you closer to your purposes? If not, how would you go about breaking the habit or replacing it with actions directed by natural law?

Why We Don't Do What's Best for Us

All of us have our own assortment of excuses for the times we don't follow our uncommon sense. And when we don't follow it, we each eventually learn the lessons of life the hard way.

For a good example, consider a scene in the movie *Scent of a Woman*, in which the main character, played by Al Pacino, is describing his experience with his uncommon sense. Pacino's character is Lt. Colonel Frank Slade, US Army, retired. During much of Slade's life, he had been a reprobate. In this scene, he was fulfilling a worthy purpose by standing up for a young friend who positively impacted his life. During that defense, Lt. Col. Slade observed—

> Now I have come to the crossroads in my life. I always knew what the right path was. Without exception, I knew, but I never took it. You know why? It was too damn hard![5]

Slade was describing what we all experience. We are aware of what our uncommon sense tells us what to do at the crossroads, but we often don't do it. We often just react to situations. Following is a partial list of the reasons (excuses?) for which we don't follow our uncommon sense:

Using Our Uncommon Sense Is Often Not What Our Immediate Appetites, Impulses, or Ego Wants

When an opportunity arises to satisfy ourselves with something we should not have or do, it takes a deliberate effort to decline. If we haven't built the habit of making a conscious decision, our natural self usually defies the natural law, what we know we should do.

It's not popular—it's an uncommon path

When we aren't living deliberately—making conscious decisions on important matters—we simply react. It's natural to let outside

---

5 *Scent of a Woman*, directed by Martin Brest, Universal Pictures, 1992.

influences affect those decisions. One of those strong influences for many people is what others think—what's popular. When our uncommon sense conflicts with what is popular, it presents quite a challenge for people who care about that social mirror.

It doesn't make complete sense to your reasoning or your emotions at the time

Your uncommon sense is not limited by your reasoning and is not emotional. It simply clarifies the natural consequences of your decisions. There are many times when your uncommon sense compels you to act before your head catches up to try to make sense out of that guidance.

In the moment, you don't care about what's right

We have all been there. A cynic may say that we all have our favorite sins, and we hold them precious. In the moment of decision, we opt for our impulse. At that point, we certainly don't want anyone else telling us what to do, especially not ourselves!

You aren't considering the long term

People are wired differently in how we consider the future. Studies show that some people are more likely to view the long-term effects of their decisions. Conversely, others are more likely to only consider the moment, or today, or this week. Your uncommon sense is geared toward the realities of your life with no time limits.

You might not have the energy to process the consequences at that moment—it just takes too much effort

There are times in each of our lives when we are stuck in survival mode. Life has beat us up and we are simply trying to summon the energy to make it through the day. In those times, it is difficult to be aware enough to even want to consider what your uncommon sense might encourage.

The people you are around don't care and you're trying to fit in

Sometimes group dynamics make standing out from the group very uncomfortable. You just want to blend in and not bring attention to yourself. The "social mirror" is more important to you than uncommon sense in that moment.

You compare yourself to others and think it's okay to not follow your instincts this time because you are doing better than they are in life

When we want to compare, we can always find someone who is doing better or worse in any area of life than we are. Of course, we are most often looking for those doing worse so we can feel better. In effect, we are saying, "I don't want to follow my uncommon sense in this situation and it's okay. I'm still doing better than they are."

No one is holding you accountable

Human nature suggests that we need to be accountable to another human in order to produce sustainable results. We too easily cease performing when we think no one else is watching. Having someone to report our results to helps motivate us.

You try to reason away your uncommon sense so you can do what you want and try to get what you want

Many of us are skilled at reasoning away our uncommon sense. Many professions even require that skill. Advertising, for example, goes to great lengths to cause us to think we need something that we don't or to do something we know we shouldn't.

Following your uncommon sense is just "too damn hard!"

Lt. Col. Frank Slade said it so well. We can just take the easiest path—the course of least resistance. However, life will beat us into submission when we defy our uncommon sense long enough. The question at that point is, will we find the energy or motivation to stop ignoring our uncommon sense for the rest of our lives?

Reasons to Follow Our Uncommon Sense

As you think about it, here is what you'll notice about your uncommon sense:

It aligns with natural law, not with how we wish the world was

Especially when we are making important decisions, many of us hope our choice will turn out positively in our favor even when that course is contrary to natural laws. Our uncommon sense doesn't rely on fantasy but on the way things really are.

It acknowledges that people, including you, will be themselves, not how we wish they would be

Some of us see the best in people. Some look for the worst. Your uncommon sense expects people to be exactly themselves in each situation.

It doesn't get caught up in the emotion of a situation

Life's important decisions are full of emotions. Your uncommon sense does not get caught up in or influenced by the emotion. Of course, when we are emotional, we have more difficulty accessing our uncommon sense. The earlier in the decision-making process that we access the uncommon sense, the clearer it will be.

It is not driven by ego—it doesn't care what others think

People who follow their uncommon sense will often not be following the crowd. That makes for good decisions, but not as many likes on social media.

It is not controlled by appetites, impulses, or habits and isn't selfish

This is probably the number one reason that people choose not to follow their uncommon sense. While it is always right in the long run, most of us are not used to disciplining ourselves consistently. It is definitely uncomfortable most of the time.

It is unlimited because it is connected to the Universe, unlike our reasoning, which is limited to our own experiences, emotions, and understanding

Once we learn to access and follow our uncommon sense, there will be times when we make decisions not knowing how every-thing will work out. We find that the outcome was beyond our comprehension at the time the decision was made. That is when we are glad that we followed that internal guidance instead of waiting until we understood the end from the beginning.

Now, is that not *truly* a superpower? To be connected with the wisdom of the Universe that follows natural law is POWER!

Reacting versus Responding to Life

Reacting to situations in life requires no deliberate effort. We allow our built-in habits, impulses, ego, or passions to determine our actions. The end result is that many times we regret reacting.

Responding instead of reacting indicates that we are putting conscious thought into the situation and making a deliberate deci-sion on how to deal with a situation that confronts us. Especially when we are trying to consciously give our uncommon sense the chance to influence us, even a brief, deliberate pause to respond in a situation allows us the opportunity to look past our reaction and to choose a path more aligned with our values.

A simple example of this can probably be found recently in a car you were driving. When other drivers triggered you by their dangerous actions and you resisted your road rage reaction of choice—whether it was to react with your vehicle or simply with the one-fingered salute—you provided an example. You resisted your angry impulse and chose a path more aligned with your intention of arriving alive at your destination.

How can you make it a habit to respond instead of react? You will need to put forth a conscious effort to identify the triggers that cause the reactions you want to change. You will need to change or "reframe" what those triggers mean to you.

For example, I do not enjoy being a hothead on the basketball court, especially since I'm playing with friends. At this point in life, I am never in a game that truly matters the second after it's over. (You could argue that I have never even been in a game that mattered!) Upon conscious evaluation, the only times I became triggered was when I disagreed with a call. I have had to reframe any such call, whether I made it or someone else did, into a decision of "would I rather preserve my relationship with my friends in the game or argue about the outcome of the call?" This analysis gives me the perspective to take a deep breath, laugh a little at myself, and get on with the game and my life.

Exercise

Think back to the habits you listed in the last exercise. How could you reframe the circumstances that cause you to indulge the habit so that you can respond instead of react?

A Drug Dealer Reconstructs His Habits

Bret was a drug dealer. His way into that life was as you might expect: he used medicinal marijuana. The weed helped him to relax and gave him an appetite for food, which he otherwise lacked. He learned about the drug and became passionate about its benefits. Then he started selling it, as well as other drugs. Now he wanted a way out, but he couldn't see how.

He had made many decisions to bring himself to this point. Each decision violated his internal guidance system—his uncommon sense—but he took the easy path to get what he wanted at the time. He justified each decision by reasoning that life had put him in the situation and this was the best option for him; he could live his own life the way he wanted. But at the same time, he was wishing that somehow the consequences of those decisions would be different for him than they were for most people.

But they weren't. He had some close friends who were also users and sellers. Some had gotten arrested, and a couple of others had died. His lifestyle finally hit home to him when he was held up at gunpoint during a drug deal. His world had closed in, and he didn't see a quick way out—or *any* way out, for that matter.

Each step he took toward becoming a drug dealer was marked by self-justifications:

- "School isn't working for me."

- "This job doesn't pay enough to support how I want to live."

- "If I do this the right way, I won't get caught."

- "I'm smarter than most, so I can make this work for me."

The contrast to each of those transitions in life would have been clarified if he had followed his uncommon sense as it led him to clearly defined purposes:

- "If I finish school, I'll have more options."

- "I have to keep this job while I find one that works better for me."

- "To stay out of jail, I have to not break the law."

- "Being smart doesn't change the consequences of natural law."

Finally realizing that natural law was not changing to accommodate his choices, Bret made the tough decision to follow his uncommon sense and change his habits and his decisions. He could then deal with reality, which kept him aligned with natural law, not the way he wished things were. This was his new method to get what he *really* wanted, even though it was slower and harder than he wanted it to be.

Now, you may or may not be a drug dealer, but the rules work the same for you as they do for Bret. This is true because you and Bret are both humans, experiencing a world that is governed by natural law.

Yes, people think all the time that they can avoid the consequences of natural law, and they sometimes seem to be right in the short term. But natural law governs and will win over time.

There is no doubt that many circumstances affecting our lives are out of our control. Uncommon sense deals with our circumstances the way they are, whatever they are. Our uncommon sense tells us, "Given the realities in your life right now, this is the path you should take."

Your uncommon sense is always—

- Dealing with reality

- Dealing with the present

- Right

So, try it out. And keep going with it . . . all the time.

Yes, since you are human, you may experience short or long periods of time that you forget or choose to not follow your uncommon sense when making a decision. Let me suggest two actions:

- Stay aware of what happens when you do and you don't do what your uncommon sense directs. Learn from those consequences.

- Come back! As soon as you want your life to be better than it is, return to the practice of allowing your uncommon sense to guide you to do what you know you should be doing with your time.

Bret's path, for example, away from the world of drug dealing has been as difficult as you might imagine, especially in the beginning. Knowing that the path would be difficult, he took two actions that have served him well.

First, he consciously thought through his life and identified all the little and big things that he would not miss and to which he did not want to return. The many stresses, the constant threat of jail, being robbed at gunpoint, friends dying and being imprisoned, the betrayals, the money uncertainties, the smells, sights, and sounds were soon imprinted in his memory.

Also on this list were the "good" things that he would have to replace and how he would replace them. The friends he knew he would lose, the lifestyle that fed his ego, and the times when cash was flowing would all have to be replaced. He developed a strategy to replace these, which served as a constant reminder of why he was taking this road.

He made the effort to change his thinking in advance so he wouldn't have to rely solely on disciplining himself along the way.

To the degree that you have to change paths in your life, you realize that the journey is definitely ever continuing and is not a destination. You will agree that it is worth that effort!

At first, you may wonder if you are simply following your own thoughts or truly your uncommon sense. Keep at it and stay aware of the results. You will answer that question yourself.

You will continually find yourself having to decide to not do some options that are good because you have better things to do. The good versus better will come from your own judgment and may change in different circumstances.

You may find that many activities that took your time in the past don't get as much of your attention anymore when you realize the difference between what you are interested in and what you can do something about. In my case, I spent a lot less time getting involved in the news and in watching sports, and more time getting off the couch and being active. I now spend more time in meaningful relationships—in a fun way!

You will enjoy being your higher self!

Exercise

For this exercise, visualize your next big crossroads decision in your life. You may be facing it immediately, or it may be in the near or distant future. Life provides many crossroads decisions. Here are a few examples:

If you are	The decision may be
In college	The career field you will pursue
Single	When/with whom you will enter a relationship
In a relationship	If/when you will have children
In a profession	If you will stay with your current role/ company/profession
Nearing retirement age	If/when you'll retire and what you will do next

Of course, most of these decisions become complex and seldom involve only one decision. For example, changing professions may be accompanied with a move, learning how to orchestrate the family dynamics, and finding what additional skills you will need to develop. To keep this exercise simple, choose only one of the decisions you would have to make.

Next, while anticipating that decision, consider the options that life is offering you today. Based on those alternatives, project out one choice you could take and describe how that could result in you being your highest self. Think about *what* you would become, not how you would do it. Record your projection, either in writing or verbally.

Here are a few questions you might ask yourself about this exercise:

continued

- What promptings do you recognize from your internal guidance system—your uncommon sense?

- What habits might you have to reconstruct to complete this action?

- What skills might you need to develop to meet the new situation?

- How would this decision result in you being your higher self?

CHAPTER 3

THE NATURAL PROCESS FOR YOUR DEVELOPMENT

If you're not sure where you are going, you're

liable to end up someplace else.

—Robert F. Mager

A s this book is being written, a big debate has been plodding along for a decade about the merits of different approaches to health care, while the most exciting aspect of health care, which isn't getting nearly as much attention, is exploding into reality, affecting the personal lives of so many people!

The field of genomics brings all of the considerations of medical science down to the individual level. Medical researchers are rapidly finding countless applications for using a person's DNA to assess what that person needs and doesn't need for their health. For example, we are now not limited to guessing or settling on a pain reliever that works for 80 percentage of the population. Each person's DNA indicates whether the pain reliever will work for them or not. The growing field of genomics opens up the possibilities of completely individualized health care that works just for you. As Dr. Karen Frieden tells us that, "Genetics dictate our tendencies for deficiencies and disease. One person's risk may be completely different than someone else's, even in their own family. If we identify these gene weaknesses, then we can prescribe nutrients, lifestyle changes, and medications so individuals can avoid disease and live their healthiest life. It's not just one-size-fits-all medicine!".

Guided by Your Uncommon Sense

An exciting parallel to individualized health care relates to your life. When your uncommon sense confirms that you have a compelling personal purpose, it's easy to get excited! You want to get on with it. You may realize that more skills may be required than you currently have, or a higher level of skill. Self-Directed Development provides you with a completely individualized approach to your growth. It's not a one-size-fits-all education!

Wanting to develop your skills when you are motivated to pursue your own compelling personal purpose is different than simply becoming more educated. You want the shortest, most efficient, and most effective path to being able to perform those skills. That path is identified by the natural laws of human performance. Here is an example of how these natural laws are applied.

Kimmie and Melissa are sisters and best friends. Melissa is a stay-at-home mom, while Kimmie is in the professional world. While discussing with each other the particular challenges they were currently facing and that were on the horizon in their individual lives, they could see that starting a business together would be the best way to address those needs.

They decided that their community in Arizona was sorely lacking a drive-through soda shop. It was a business opportunity they could get excited about. They were both aware of the benefits of following their internal guidance—their uncommon sense—and recognized its influence in this direction for their lives.

They both have bachelor's degrees, but their studies in social work and communications hadn't adequately prepared them to be entrepreneurial business moguls. They assessed their combined skills against the skills that would be required of them and made a list. That list became part of their business plan.

They needed a systematic plan for developing certain skills, so they followed these steps:

1. They first determined who would be responsible for the tasks that required specific skills.

2. They were then able to assign who would bring those skills to the business.

3. Some skills they would choose to hire, such as tax accounting, finding potential employees, and web design

and maintenance. They were still clear on which one of them would be responsible for each task and its related skills.

4. For the skills they each needed to develop, they clearly defined the objectives.

5. With the objectives clear, they started their search for performance-based skills training on YouTube. They could achieve the objectives of many of the skills they needed from YouTube or other skills-training programs they could find online.

6. For the remaining skills, they found subject matter experts who were willing to help them, sometimes for a price or for a trade of services.

7. Since they each had instructional design skills, they were able to structure training modules using the subject matter experts' input.

8. They agreed to hold each other accountable for the tasks assigned and the results of their efforts. They also agreed on how each would be held accountable.

Their skills training followed the most efficient and effective path so they could get their business running. Why do you think they didn't return to school to develop the skills they needed? They didn't want to spend that much time and money!

Kimmie and Melissa's choice is not an insult to education. Public/private education plays a different role in our society than skills development. The focus of each is different. The focus of

Kimmie and Melissa's plan was to learn skills that they would use immediately. Instead of using education to develop the required skills, the program they used is called Self-Directed Development. Its roots are in a field of corporate training called "performance-based training."

One of the pioneers of performance-based training was a human behavioral scientist named Dr. Robert Mager. While there are other noteworthy pioneers in this field, it was Dr. Mager's science-based criterion-referenced instruction (CRI) methodology that the Air Force used to develop its undergraduate pilot training. In fact, the CRI methodology has been translated into sixteen languages and is used all over the world, in every industry of business.

Dr. Mager's CRI provides something you probably need once you identify your compelling personal purposes. When you need to develop new skills or need to further develop skills you already have, you can use his methodology described in this chapter as the shortest path to get there. It's simple, so be prepared for a blinding flash of the obvious.

There are five components in performance-based training that you need for effectively developing any skill: (1) clear, objective objectives; (2) relevant information; (3) processes to learn; (4) practice and feedback; and (5) ways to check your skills.

1. Clear, Objective Objectives

The first step is creating clear, objective objectives. The word *objective* is repeated intentionally. The skill you need to develop should be described in the objective by a verb of observable action. Examples would be as follows:

- Negotiate contracts with terms favorable to your business.

- Create objective job descriptions.

- Write sentences without errors in spelling and punctuation.

Those actions can all be observed. Using a verb of unobservable action—such as *know*, *understand*, or *appreciate*—leaves the objective subjective, so how does one know when the goal is met? Avoid using these subjective verbs of ephemeral action in an objective. The performance for which the knowledge, understanding, or appreciation will be used should be the target of the objective.

2. Relevant Information

You need *relevant* information. When you finish the sentence "I can't start practicing until I know _____," you will have defined all of the relevant information you need to have. Notice that you don't need all of the information available on the topic; you only need enough knowledge to allow you to start practicing the task.

For example, if the task is changing a car tire, I don't need information on the history of tires and wheels. I don't need to know which wheels are best. That information is not relevant to me performing the task.

I may need to know if certain wheels need special care during the tire-changing process because of the alloy from which they are made. I may also need to know what a torque wrench is. That is relevant information.

3. Processes to Learn

You need instruction on processes you don't yet know how to perform. When you finish the sentence "I can't start practicing until I know how to _____," you will have identified the process(es) you need to learn in order to master the skill.

For example, if the task is to change a car tire while on the side of the road, I may need to know all of the steps in the process from the time I remove the tire jack from the trunk until the tire is changed and the flat tire is stored back in the trunk. I may also need to know the processes for loosening and tightening lug nuts.

4. Practice and Feedback

Then you must practice the skill—crucially, while receiving feedback. "Practice makes perfect" is only true when you are getting feedback on your practice. Practice without feedback is a good way to learn to do something the wrong way. Practicing with feedback until you can perform the skill is irreplaceable. This is why simply studying about the skill is not enough. I wouldn't allow someone to perform surgery on me when their knowledge was limited to reading about it!

Hands-on practice with feedback is arguably the most essential component in skills training. It is also the most tragically ignored component. People have a hard time allowing for adequate practice and feedback, somehow thinking that practice will happen naturally as the person is performing for real. Unfortunately, people do often learn by practicing in a real situation. But it's an ineffective and expensive way to learn a skill. A person needs practice and feedback until ready for the skill check.

5. Ways to Check Your Skills

Finally, you need a skill check. Ideally, you should perform the task for a competent authority who can validate that you did it correctly. The validation helps to give you the confidence that you will be able to perform that skill when it counts.

Now, relate these five steps to skills you have already developed. You probably recognize most, if not all, of the steps as part of your skills development. You undoubtedly recognize the value of completing all five steps as part of the process you need to develop the skills required to fulfill your compelling personal purposes.

You probably also recognize that while these are the five steps required for any skills development *process*, more steps will be required for you to have a complete plan for your own development. That complete system is called your "Self-Directed Development."

More About Your Self-Directed Development

Kimmie and Melissa, the entrepreneurs from the beginning of this chapter, used this five-step system to ensure they learned all the skills they needed to run their business. Since Self-Directed Development is individually tailored for each participant, use their example as a guide to determine what it is and how it would work for *you*. Although everyone has experienced *some* components of this approach, you likely have not experienced the *complete* system. Here are the skills you need in order to get the greatest benefit from that system:

- Accessing your uncommon sense

- Establishing your compelling personal purposes

- Identifying the skills you need to develop

- Developing performance objectives to use in evaluating your skills training

- Establishing your Self-Directed Development plan

- Finding or developing the skills training required by your plan

- Using a development advisor as a resource to progress through your plan

You may have seen components of Self-Directed Development in public schools, universities, trade schools, private schools, corporate training, and any number of human performance programs. All human performance efforts should, and do, overlap. The difference is that Self-Directed Development is based completely on the science of human performance—natural law. It uses Dr. Mager's CRI methodology as the most efficient and effective way to develop skills. The science behind it ensures that no resources are spent on anything other than skill development.

The purpose of Self-Directed Development is to focus on each particular skill you want to learn rather than on tangential or unrelated topics. In contrast, you probably have spent hours in classes learning material that relates to nothing you will ever do, wondering why you were even there.

There is no path or program laid out for you in Self-Directed Development; the system is literally self-directed. For example, no school curriculum is established for you. You need a curriculum—a path—that fits you exactly, so you have to do that work yourself, just as Kimmie and Melissa did in our example.

Many people have never thought about personal development in terms of *skills* and have never developed a learning program around their own skills development. Directing your own improvement may be a new experience, but you can use the parameters laid out in this chapter, and there are many resources available to help you in those efforts.

Exercise

Think of a skill you'd like to learn, such as bookkeeping, investing in cryptocurrency, or starting a conversation with a stranger that is meaningful for them. It doesn't need to be professional development; it can be anything that takes you a step closer to a compelling personal purpose. Keep it simple for this exercise.

Skill: _____

Now, let's start with why you want to learn this skill. How does it align with your purpose? Write down your answer here or on a sheet of paper.

_____

What people do you know or know of who might help you develop this skill and provide feedback to you?

_____

_____

Once your objective is clearly established, where might you search to find the skill training that will result in you being able to perform the skill as you need to?

_____

_____

_____

As you search for assistance to develop your skill, you will find many resources available. One such resource is Your Uncommon Path Foundation.

Your Uncommon Path Foundation's version of Self-Directed Development

Your Uncommon Path Foundation is a nonprofit resource that has been established to help people master life's transitions. The foundation's version of Self-Directed Development begins with the participant taking a two-day facilitated training session called Crossroads Decisions Process.

The point of this training session is to ensure you have all of the skills required to pursue your Self-Directed Development and to create your individualized plan. With a plan in place, you are ready to set off on your own down your road less traveled. You now know where you are going and what you will have to do to get there.

Anyone can participate in Self-Directed Development at any point in their life.

You do not have to be involved with the foundation in order to participate in Self-Directed Development. The foundation has some free resources and some services for pay, none of which are required for you to be successful at developing the skills you need for your purposes.

The Essential Role of an Advisor

Of course, no example will fit your situation exactly. You need to create your *own* Self-Directed Development plan to develop only the skills you need to allow you to fulfill compelling personal purposes that are your own, validated by the only judge that matters—your conscience!

You also need the help of an advisor. You are a human. One of the natural laws of human performance over a period of time is that you need to be accountable to another human. For our purposes here, that other human is your advisor.

You should care more about your success than anyone else does, but some days don't seem like that. Your advisor needs to care enough to step into that role when you are not feeling it. You may need several people helping you to be successful. The advisor is one you will probably need the most often.

The title "advisor" is used deliberately instead of coach, guide, or mentor. All of these are perfectly good titles, but one of the most important traits you need in this person is that he/she can resist the temptation of telling you what to do. "Advisor" suggests someone who can ask helpful questions and provide information but who doesn't give you orders.

To qualify as an advisor for your Self-Directed Development, a person must have the following prerequisite skills. They must be able to—

- Redirect you to your uncommon sense in a way that you will accept, not tell you what to do

- Hold you accountable in a way to which you respond constructively

- Help you derive performance objectives and skill checks and to identify valid skills training

- Assist you in recognizing/describing skills

- Assist in establishing and adjusting your Self-Directed Development plan

A few comments on these skills are appropriate here.

Redirect you to your uncommon sense, not tell you what to do . . .

When you have a trusted advisor in any field, you can easily fall into the trap of allowing the advisor to tell you what to do. When we are in the trusted advisor role, we easily fall into the trap of telling others what they should do. Both are traps. Both result in our not doing the required work to access our uncommon sense for guidance. We are then living a piece of someone *else's* life. We are not living deliberately.

As difficult as it may be, the advisor must only refer you back to your uncommon sense to answer the question "What should I do?" The advisor, or anyone else, can help you determine how to do it, but your uncommon sense should be the one to tell you "what" to do.

I was sitting near the hot tub of our community facility one day when I overheard a tremendous example of a helpful advisory role.

An older gentleman was enjoying the hot tub when a twenty-something-year-old slid into the water and started talking about his extreme woes.

The monologue continued more than ten minutes as the young man poured out his sad tales of being victimized by circumstances, roommates, bosses, teachers, and his parents. The older gentleman didn't interrupt, nor did he try to get a word in. After the extended rant, the young man finally realized that he had provoked no reaction, so he paused after asking, "You seem experienced in life; what do you think I should do?"

"You would like my input?" confirmed the man.

"Sure."

"I think your conscience can guide you. You already know what to do," was the simple response.

"I do? What?"

"I don't know. Your inner guidance talks to *you*, not to me."

"Well, what do you suggest, based on your experience?" countered the young man.

"I don't have any experience being you, being in your situations, and receiving guidance from your conscience. That is customized guidance just for you. Do you already know exactly what you should do when you listen to that guidance?"

"I guess so, but I want to learn from the best experience from others."

"No one else can tell you what you should do. They don't have any experience that tells you what you should do. They may have experience to share on how to do things, but you are the only one responsible for what you do. It has to come from you and be your decision."

"Well, my parents think I should follow this certain path," persisted the young man.

"Fine, but follow your conscience," was the sage's reply.

The following ten minutes was a broken record of the young man stating what others thought, countered by the sage saying, "Fine, but follow your conscience."

Finally, the older man felt overdone by the hot water and rose to leave. The young man, acknowledging that the lesson had sunk in, said, "Can I get your name? This is probably the most useful advice I have ever received!"

The sage replied, "Good, but it's all I've got for you. The message won't change."

"Might I find you here at the hot tub again? Could we talk some more?"

"That could happen, but my input to you won't change and won't get any more profound. Follow your conscience. That's all I've got."

In that twenty-minute interaction, I had observed one of the greatest lessons of life that young man and I had and will ever receive.

Hold you accountable

An essential element of living deliberately is taking responsibility for your decisions and actions. When you determine your own compelling personal purpose and formulate a plan for achieving it, no one else has the responsibility for taking the actions necessary to fulfill your purpose.

All humans need another human to hold them accountable for their commitments and their actions. That includes you. Your advisor must be uniquely qualified to hold you accountable in a way to which you will respond constructively. That is determined by the two of you. You must agree how you will be held accountable for each commitment and for each action.

Derive performance objectives from skills

Both you and your advisor must have the skill of deriving performance objectives from skills. You learn this skill in the Crossroads Decisions Training that is a prerequisite for Self-Directed Development.

The advisor helps you to write and use the performance objectives. The objectives are then used to identify necessary skills training. Skills training is valid only when it results in you developing the skill you need.

Developing the specific skill you need is important because many courses, classes, and trainings are patterned after the academic model. They provide information about the subject but don't allow the participant to practice the skill and receive immediate feedback. Such trainings also don't usually require a participant to then demonstrate proficiency in the skill to a qualified person who can validate it. *You need to be sure you have the skill, not just information about the skill. The performance objective is the key to achieving that.*

Assist you to identify skills

Most of us require training to be able to correctly identify the skills required to meet a specific goal. Some skills are obvious, but many are not. The "soft skills," especially, are often overlooked.

Soft skills are generally the people skills required for effective human interaction. Skills such as developing trust, communicating effectively, managing people, leading people, and having a positive attitude are all examples of soft skills. Soft skills are always involved in people being successful. Your advisor ensures that you identify all the skills required for you to be successful, not only the obvious ones.

Exercise

Now let's return to the Self-Directed Development exercise from earlier. Who do you know who might make a good advisor on your path to learning this skill? Remember, you want someone—

- Who will direct you to find the best solution for you, not tell you what to do

- Who will hold you accountable

- Who will help you define and establish learning objectives

---

continued

> • Who will help you identify new skills
>
> Your Uncommon Path Foundation has a training program that will help a person develop these skills at no charge.

Everyone with These Life Skills Could/ Should Be an Advisor

When Your Uncommon Path Foundation conducts the before-mentioned Crossroads Decisions Training, a common reaction among established adults is, "I'm already pretty good with most of these skills, but my child/grandchild/friend/sibling/coworkers/ acquaintances *really* need this!" Our response to that reaction is a version of, "Good! Teach it to them and be their advisor." (With the exception of your own children. Most of the time they need to be advised by someone other than their parent.)

If someone has developed the skills of following their uncommon sense, recognizing their compelling personal purposes, identifying skills required to be successful in life, and partnering with a person to hold them accountable, they should be teaching and advising this material. People can get help from the foundation on the other skill required of an advisor—namely, deriving performance objectives from skills.

The skills of being successful in life that everyone needs are different from the skills required in specific professions or avocations. The people who can identify specific professional skills are subject-matter experts. They play a role, but that is not required of advisors.

The skills to be successful in life are not easily observed and are not objectively measured. They are referred to as "soft skills." These soft skills include the people skills that allow you to interact effectively with others. They also include skills such as judgment, critical thinking, problem-solving, decision-making, and teamwork. These skills are always in demand and are often overlooked by people trying to develop themselves for accomplishing their compelling personal purposes. This is why you qualify as an advisor if you have these skills. The experience and insights of a person who has developed these skills in life is such a valuable resource for someone pursuing Self-Directed Development.

Especially if your crossroads transition in life, like retirement, has allowed you the time to pursue meaningful contributions, helping others in this way might be quite rewarding for you. One excellent example of this positive contribution is by my friend Dr. Dick Harper.

Dick had a successful career as a clinical psychologist. He started that career in the US Air Force, then transitioned into running a private business-consulting practice with the help of his administratively skilled wife. His practice started with a broad clientele of anyone who needed his service and became more focused over time to assist small entrepreneurial and family businesses in succession strategies for passing the business on to the next generation. In his transition to retirement, he had many interests to pursue, one of which will continue to provide him meaning and purpose as long as he has breath and capacity.

Dick spends time helping people fulfill their own "hero's journey" by acting as an advisor for them. The phrase comes from Joseph Campbell's published works in applying topics on mythology that relate to our lives.

People are on their hero's journey when they reach a point in their life of realizing the deep desire to "give back" or to "pay forward" what they have been gifted in life. He does this by meeting with mentees as regularly as they choose and sharing conversation and insights from his vast experience with people and from his impressive studies of human history and the human condition. He does this in a loving way and strives to learn from his mentees as well.

Dick is an example of the rich reservoir of skills that most everyone needs to be successful in life in addition to their specialized professional skills. Those soft skills that successful people have developed can help others. There is always an avenue that life will offer you to help other people with the many success skills that you have developed.

Can Kids Self-Direct?

Up to this point, this chapter has been talking about adults doing their own Self-Directed Development, which is completely appropriate. But sooner or later, you may find yourself wondering whether kids can do it too, and to what degree.

Well, as it happens, two of my granddaughters can. Lucy is eleven and Lydia is nine, and they are pursuing their own Self-Directed Development program, in addition to attending their regular school.

One interesting note: they, by their own choice, don't call it "Self-Directed Development." Instead, they came up with their *own* name for the program: "You Decide Education" or "UDecidEd."

They may have chosen a different name, but they are still taking the *same path* anyone else takes. They started by completing the

Crossroads Decisions Training and demonstrated that they could, indeed, follow their uncommon sense and define compelling personal purposes for themselves.

Focusing on these purposes, Lucy and Lydia broke down the skills they would need to develop. They each are required to be working on two skills at a time so if progress stalls on one, they can move to the other.

After selecting their skills, they recruited their development advisors from people who had been trained in the skills required of advisors. It's best for a participant's parent, regardless of background qualifications, to not be the advisor. Lucy was able to recruit Mema (her grandmother), and Lydia recruited her uncle Chris, both of whom have been trained as advisors.

So now, from this point, let's observe their individual development process to date . . .

Lucy is interested in possibly running a day care facility at some point in her life, so she thought it wise to develop her babysitting skills, possibly turning that into a business. After considering the many skills she would need to develop, she settled on starting with two that related to her babysitting:

- Talking with adults about money, as it relates to babysitting

- Handling the various emergencies that could occur while she was babysitting

Lucy's next step was to find a subject matter expert (SME) for each skill. She could have easily asked her mom to be the

SME for the babysitting-related skills, but she ventured out to ask another mom who uses babysitters regularly.

While preparing to interview the SMEs, Lucy had her advisor give her input on questions to ask, as well as what information she would need to have in order to recognize adequate skills training if she found it, or to have the training developed. Both SMEs were impressed with Lucy's preparation.

With the skill requirements clearly defined by the SMEs, Lucy's next job was to write the performance objective for each skill. That performance objective would be used to evaluate any skills training that Lucy found. Since Lucy has not yet been trained in writing performance objectives, her advisor worked with her to complete them.

Then it was time to find the training for Lucy to develop the skills she wanted. She found many sources of information, including some classes, but only one class that matched her *objectives*. You see, even though a class might provide information on the subject, if it doesn't allow Lucy to practice the skill and get feedback, and then to perform a skill check for an SME, it wouldn't help her. She wanted, and needed, to have specific skills when she finished the class, not just information.

The two babysitting objectives required training to be developed for them, since Lucy couldn't find existing training that met those objectives. She approached her aunt, who had the skills and developed the training for her at no charge. With that, Lucy was on her own path to Self-Directed Development.

In the not-too-distant future, Lucy envisions a business in which she has several girls her age who are certified in the skills of babysitting, complete with certificates that have the skills listed.

Parents will be able to make just one call, to Lucy, to find a qualified, available babysitter. They will pay a fair rate, a small portion of which goes to Lucy, while the babysitters get paid fairly and have regular work. One of the biggest perks to Lucy is not only the income, but also being able to afford her own phone, which is also a business expense!

Lydia impressed her advisor right away by choosing three skills:

- Baking desserts

- Eating healthy

- Establishing an exercise program for good health

She explained that the two skills relating to health were mostly for her but could also turn into a business for a personal coaching program for kids' health. Baking the desserts would be an easy way for her to both earn money and to find people who might need a personal coach for kids' health.

The SMEs were easy for Lydia to find. She had a family member who could bake several unique and delicious desserts and was glad to work with her. Her advisor was also a health-conscious dad of his own kids who was interested in those subjects and would be glad to help.

The costs were minimal for Lydia, and the initial work of building a training was also done by her aunt. So Lydia was quickly off and running!

In the not-too-distant future, Lydia envisions being healthy and having two diversified but complementary businesses. The unique desserts will provide income. Parents concerned about health will pay Lydia as a kids' health coach to have their children develop healthy and interesting menus, as well as an exercise program.

Accountability

The difficulty Lucy and Lydia have with UDecidEd is that they are people. People of any age have a hard time staying motivated when the required activity turns into real effort. That is why all humans need to be accountable to another person. The advisor plays a key role.

Lydia's and Lucy's advisors are adults. Since adults easily resort to the role of authority figures, the advisor-training program requires advisors to demonstrate the skill of *not* telling participants what to do . . . EVER! Advisors can hold participants accountable, which is essential, but only in the time and the way that the participants want. The participants decide. The participants also decide when and how often to work on their skills. The advisors don't hound them to get it done. The participants don't have to participate. People learn when and what they want to learn!

What keeps them going?

The advisor plays a key role, but accountability alone doesn't keep people going. People need rewards. Rewards are "in the eye of the rewardee." What I may think is a reward may be a punishment to *you*. For example, I can be rewarded with a good, crisp apple with peanut butter on it. You, on the other hand, might find that disgusting.

Each participant of Self-Directed Development must

determine their rewards, as well as when they need to be rewarded to maintain progress.

Lucy, for example, may be excited about running her own babysitting business, but that can seem so far off to the eleven-year-old that it is not enough to keep her motivated daily as she works on the seemingly endless list of twenty-four skills she needs to develop. Therefore, Lucy devised some rewards that excite her as she goes.

UDecidEd rewards Lucy with a professional certificate upon completion of a group of skills. That's a good midrange reward. She also needs shorter-range rewards. She convinced her mom to provide a grab bag. That is simply a bag full of cheap items that Lucy enjoys—jewelry, gadgets, treats, and pre-makeup beautifiers (whatever that means). As Lucy completes a skill check for each skill along the way, she gets to reach in the grab bag and pull out a reward. It's a simple system that Lucy designed for Lucy, and it works.

Lydia is motivated differently and therefore has developed a different system. While some elements are similar to Lucy's, Lydia uses her reward system to get things done as part of her progress in UDecidEd. She has negotiated with her advisor, her parents, and some other family members for their cooperation in providing things for her. For example, she approached her dad with the deal of "if I complete this skill by this date, will you provide the ingredients I need for the next skill?" That works to keep her motivated and going.

The point, of course, is that *everyone* needs a reward system that works for *them*. In Self-Directed Development, as in Lucy and Lydia's UDecidEd, the participant is responsible for establishing their own reward system, and for adjusting it if/when it stops working for them.

Age?

Age has little to do with kids' self-directing. Some can do it while they're still quite young. Some can't do it even as adults . . . okay, that's probably too cynical, but the point is that people can be involved in Self-Directed Development when they recognize that they have skills they want to develop. They also must have the skill of allowing themselves to be accountable. That may happen at age seven or seventy!

The Natural Laws in Self-Directed Development

While many versions and interpretations of skills training exist, in order to achieve your purposes, Self-Directed Development includes some essential elements that few, if any, skills-training programs include.

To clarify, the process you follow in Self-Directed Development is illustrated here:

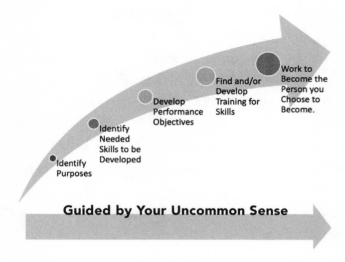

1. You are guided by your uncommon sense throughout the process.

2. You identify your compelling personal purposes that motivate you.

3. You identify all of the skills you need to develop further.

4. You develop a performance objective for each skill—this is the foundation of your Self-Directed Development Plan.

5. You find, or have developed, the training for each skill that will result in achieving the performance objective.

6. You advance in the training by demonstrating competence in each required skill as you work your tail off to become the person you choose to become.

The most essential of the components that is required to achieve your compelling personal purposes in life is that you be guided by your uncommon sense throughout. You are trying to achieve something that few people achieve to their own satisfaction. You are moving beyond living a normal life. You are accepting guidance from the wisdom of the Universe. Fortunately, wisdom is always available to you—at no financial cost. You need only to stay consciously aware of common sense through whatever routines, habits, and/or rituals you develop for yourself.

As your purposes evolve, clarify, and become increasingly important to you, you will still need to exert effort to refrain from stalling or giving up. Your efforts are for a lifetime, and you are running a marathon. You will need to consciously and deliberately establish your compelling personal purposes and to stay aware of them through the clutter of life. An advisor is necessary to fulfill the critical function of guiding you when you need it.

Part of your clutter of life is what other people have decided your purposes are, and what you need to do to achieve them. A person can live their entire life without giving thought to their purposes or skills, since the pathway of schools, jobs, family, retirement, and death are a ready-made part of life. None of those are necessarily "bad." You just have to make your own deliberate decisions if you are going to achieve your purposes, your way!

Most people think in terms of schooling instead of directing their own learning. Since that is the norm, your focus on skills training may seem unnatural, especially when others aren't doing it as you are. Many won't understand your efforts or your motives. You will truly be on the road less traveled when you are pursuing skills training the way Self-Directed Development requires.

There are no age requirements for Self-Directed Development, so any individual can participate as long as they can perform the prerequisites of—

- Establishing their compelling personal purposes

- Working with an advisor to establish and accomplish their skills-training plan

- Arranging for the people, training, and financial resources required by their plan

Exercise

Now what? What are the next three steps you should take toward your own development in order to pursue your compelling personal purposes? Record your answers in the space below or in another place, video, or audio.

_____

_____

_____

CHAPTER 4

AT THE CROSSROADS OF LIFE

Two roads diverged in a wood, and I—

I took the one less traveled by,

And that has made all the difference.

—Robert Frost

We have all been making crossroads decisions since before even realizing it. Those are the decisions we make in life that have a big impact on what happens in our future, sometimes for the rest of our lives.

For example, early in life we chose friends without even considering the future impact. We also decided when to make our own decisions independent of our parents' input. Many of those decisions built habits that affected our mental and physical health for years to come. In some cases, we still live with the effects of those decisions.

We probably started recognizing how important some of those decisions were about the time we were deciding how long to endure structured education and what to do after that. From that point on, we can understand the image of being at the crossroads of life, realizing that the big decisions we make will determine a direction that will change our life. When we stand at a crossroads, we face paths (decisions) that take us different directions to different destinations. These are arguably the most important decisions we'll make, and they're often the hardest.

We don't all have the same crossroads decisions in life, though we have many in common. Common crossroads decisions can include the following:

- Choosing a life partner

- Choosing a career

- Deciding on changing a career

- Choosing to move locations

- Having a family

- Choosing to go to college or not

- Choosing a college or educational institution

- Deciding when to retire

- Choosing what to do after retiring

- Choosing friends

- Choosing investments

- Buying a home or renting

And this list can continue on . . .

Many of us feel the weight of the world when faced with these decisions because they *do* impact our lives. They *are* important and often daunting decisions. This chapter suggests a new way to approach those decisions, or at least reminds us of a way that many of us have long forgotten.

The internal tools we have for making decisions boil down to two basics: brains and emotions. We use both during our crossroads decision-making. Most of us are geared to use one more than the other. The input we receive from our brains is limited to what we have deposited, as is the input from our emotions.

The typical response for most of us who see a big life decision approaching is to start gathering data or information. Perhaps we sense our vulnerability since our own data to date is severely limited. In any case, we begin to research and to get input from others.

Why would we not access our uncommon sense first?

Using Your Uncommon Sense

While this book was being written, my wife and I bought a house after living in my sister's basement paying rent for eleven years. I've enjoyed the sympathy I get from people when I've told them that I live in my sister's basement, until those people see it. It's a *really* nice basement.

We surprised ourselves eleven years ago by moving into the basement when we had a perfectly good home nearby. This choice was presented to us by our uncommon sense. We didn't have any logical or emotional reasons for moving there. We thought we would live there for a few months. We came up with some logical-sounding reasons so we could explain to our incredulous friends and family why we were making the move. But we knew that we didn't truly know why. We both recognized the guidance from our uncommon sense, and that was good enough for us. We couldn't quite explain it, but we have found it has always been in our best interests to follow that uncommon sense.

After eleven years of compiling numerous purposes served by living there, we found ourselves in the same situation when we made the choice to purchase a new home and move nearby. When the situation suddenly presented itself, we first weighed the option of moving or staying put against our individual and combined purposes. Realizing that the initial purposes that led us there had been fulfilled, and that moving would not prevent any of our existing purposes, we felt either option would be good. Our "sense," however, was that we should go ahead and make the move.

We both knew it was the right move, but the decision was driven by our uncommon sense. Since we couldn't really explain that to others, we had to identify some valid-sounding reasons from our logic and emotions that may or may not have been part of the decision-making, but they made sense to us and allowed us to have an explanation for others.

That is essentially the process of using your uncommon sense to make the crossroads decisions in your life. When you first face the possibility of the decision, you simply make yourself aware that you are about to take a big step and then ask yourself what you should do. Weigh the options against the purposes you have already defined in life. Do not start the analytical lists yet, and do not allow yourself the emotions that will come. Stay aware of your uncommon sense. It will give you guidance the same way it has your entire life. Allow yourself to recognize it.

If you are making the decision with another person, the discussion should simply be around your purposes and the direction you should take, not about the pros and cons or about how you feel about making the decision. Once you agree on the path you should take, *then* allow your head and reasoning to catch up and also experience the emotions.

Using Only Your Brains/Reasoning/Logic

You know your brain is engaged when you analytically consider the options. You may even make lists of the pros and cons of the decisions, sometimes assigning points to various items on the list.

For example, during the new COVID-influenced professional world, many people have the option of living wherever they choose while they work virtually. I spoke with several clients who wanted to take advantage of the options. The process was basically the same for all of them. They listed all possible locations they would consider, then narrowed their list down to the five most likely locations. They then listed the ten main considerations such as weather, cost of living, safety, schools, and so on. They were getting insights from as many people as they could, along with info they could gather online, relying on the lists to clarify their decision.

Of course, the limitations with using this approach include the fact that your reasoning is limited to your experiences and capacity. When you request the input of others, they have those same limitations. Even the all-knowing internet has limitations on the insights it can give you, especially when you consider that the internet doesn't have to live with the consequences of your decision!

The problem with using only this analytical approach is that it can lead people to find somewhere that checks off every item on their list but then disappoints for any number of reasons, such as any of the family members not finding friends in the new location.

Using Only Your Emotions

The value of the emotions that go into your decision-making depends largely on the source of those emotions. That's a pretty murky subject. When the weight of the decision increases, the volume and complexities of the emotions also increase. That certainly doesn't clarify the decision, but for most of us, it pushes us to conclusions.

In the world of professional selling is a commonly held belief that people buy based on emotion, then rationalize their buying decisions with logic. Of course, the limitation of that approach is overlooking some important features or settling for something less and regretting it later.

The Source of Clarity

The important point here is to not begin the big crossroads decisions with either your reasoning or with your emotions. Instead, begin those decisions against the backdrop of your compelling personal purpose and in harmony with your uncommon sense.

That dynamic duo of your purpose and your uncommon sense will clarify your decision. *Then*, your brains and your emotions will demand to weigh in, and you want them to, but they have specific roles.

Once your uncommon sense confirms a decision that aligns with your compelling personal purpose, your brain needs to make sense of it, and your emotions need to reach peace with it. You need both your brains and emotions as you determine *how* to proceed once you have established *where* to go.

Remember the story of twenty-year-old pregnant Kailey? We can all see how impossibly difficult that decision could be for those who don't have the benefit of a clear purpose before all of the emotions and well-meaning advice come crashing in like an avalanche from the many people who don't have to live with the consequences.

Even if the practice of starting one's crossroads decisions with uncommon sense and compelling personal purpose seems like common sense, people often don't make decisions this way.

Follow Your Own Path

In a retirement community, compelling personal purposes, or the lack of such, are on full display. Many people choose to retire "because it's time" without consideration of how that aligns with their purposes in life. It's easy to fall into that trap because retirement is expected around a certain age or scenario in life. The path is often established by others.

The problem is when all of the effort is made to retire *from* something without considering what you are retiring *to*. In these cases, retirement is so "we can relax and play golf," or whatever other generality is used to describe the bliss. In that case, retirees play a lot of golf in a short amount of time before realizing that they have much more time available than the activities fill. Retired friends often ask each other, "How do you fill the time?" That is an indication that the retirement decision was made without considering personal purposes.

An equally perplexing problem is when the professional role is mistaken as the sole purpose of life. For example, as Marshall transitioned into retirement after being CEO of a multinational corporation, he accepted the invitation to sit on the board of directors for his company and for one other. Traveling between Arizona and Northern Europe for meetings and events became burdensome to both him and his wife, Nancy. But he kept accepting renewal offers and positions on other boards. During the strain on both his marriage and his health, he admitted in confidence that he kept doing it because he couldn't stand the thought of becoming irrelevant. In other words, he didn't recognize compelling personal purposes beyond his professional career.

People often confuse the activities in their lives with who they are and what their purposes are in life. Purposes don't stop with a big change in life, not even with retirement. Our "relevance" in the world comes from the person we are, not the activities in our life.

Bob and Eileen Mager set a good example of pursuing one's own purposes or establishing one's own path. They met in their professional field of corporate training while Bob was becoming world renowned, and Eileen was established in her own right. Later in life, when they felt it was time to leave that field, they shifted gears and turned their attention and efforts to other pursuits that interested them. That's who they were—and Eileen still is.

What they created depended on the circumstances in life, but they always had purposes because the world always needs creation. Bob pursued several interests; the most compelling was writing mystery novels. Eileen continued developing her musical talents and performed for thousands of people. They seldom talked about their accomplishments in their past professional field, even though they had gained celebrity status there. They had moved on and were happily following their mantra of "do something."

The message from these examples is that there are always purposes in your life. Begin each new journey with your purposes firmly established. Your uncommon sense helps to guide you with that.

You Make Your Own Decisions

If you were rating the difficulty of crossroads decisions like we rate college football teams, perhaps the number one most difficult decision would be choosing the person you want to spend the rest of your life with. Combining the potential impact on your life with all of the emotions involved adds to the normal complexities of big decisions. That is why Rick was approaching the decision with the attitude of allowing God to make his decision.

Everything was falling into place as it should. When he first saw Celeste at age fifteen, he was thunderstruck and knew that he would marry her. It was fate. Circumstances prevented them from dating until college, but as the end of college was in sight, they started dating and the next step was naturally to get married just as Rick had envisioned.

With all of the circumstances lined up, Rick was sure of what was happening but wanted something more. He wanted confirmation from his uncommon sense that this was the right move. In a way, he wanted his uncommon sense to make the decision.

He arranged for some alone time in the most distraction-free environment he knew so he could access his uncommon sense in earnest. While in that contemplative state, sincerely trying to search past his ego and emotions, he claims to have actually heard a voice. He says he didn't think anyone was there, but he looked around, just to be sure.

The voice said simply, "Make your own decision!"

He thought that to be strange guidance. At that point in life, he thought God, fate, or "the powers that be" would make decisions for him through his uncommon sense. But that's not how it works in a world governed by natural law. In this world, nothing absolves us from the consequences of the decisions we make. Thus, we have to make those decisions.

Our uncommon sense guides us by helping us recognize the consequences of our decisions. It brings clarity, but the decisions are still ours.

With this new perspective, Rick had to acknowledge that he shouldn't get married to anyone at that point. He realized that he was not ready for the commitments and the selflessness required for the type of marriage he wanted. He knew his ego was in the way and he was too proud and impulsive. He had some internal work to do before getting married. That was the clarity provided by his uncommon sense. He made his decision by passing on the chance to ask Celeste to marry him.

Who lives with the consequences of each of our decisions? While other people are affected by some of our decisions, *we* must live with the consequences of all our decisions. Who is responsible for those decisions? No one else but us! Doesn't it align best with natural law for the person responsible and required to live with the consequences to make the decision?

The message from this story is to seek the clarity of the consequences of your decisions when at the crossroads. Your uncommon sense provides that clarity.

Others May Not Understand Your Path

When Courtney accepted Mike's marriage proposal, she knew of his involvement with drugs and gangs in the past. She was impressed with his attempts to stay clean and live a mainstream life.

Beginning on the day of the wedding, the early indicators were ominous when several people noticed that Mike was high on something. During the honeymoon he disappeared for a few hours, then came back telling of how he was mugged and got lost chasing the culprits after all of the money gifted to them at the wedding reception was stolen.

The first breaking point was when Mike staged a robbery at the home in which he and Courtney were staying as guests. A new credit card was stolen, and $1,000 cash withdrawn on it. Of course, a drug addict doesn't always act with clarity of thought, so when the call for the withdrawal was traced to Mike's phone, Courtney had confirmation on what she instinctively knew. Mike's involvement with drugs was not in the past.

To Courtney's friends and family, Mike's drug use was a clear opportunity for her to have the wedding annulled and to move on with her life. She didn't. Neither did she defend Mike but tried valiantly to stay with him to support him in getting the professional help he needed. Friends and family despaired at her apparent co-dependency, but one by one, those friends and family started realizing that Courtney was acting from a position of strength, not weakness.

What was giving Courtney that strength? She did not know how it would turn out, but Courtney was deliberately allowing her uncommon sense to guide her decisions. Virtually every day brought a new crossroads decision.

Courtney's purpose in the relationship became giving Mike the best chance he would probably ever have in his life to finally quit the drugs and live a purpose-driven life. Through the pain and uncertainties, she sought and did her best to follow that uncommon sense that, she believed, was right, was not involved in the emotion, and was connected to the wisdom of the Universe. Of course, her path brought tremendous challenges and the accompanying roller coaster of emotions. People who didn't understand her decisions constantly questioned her actions. She kept clarity by staying focused on her purpose while making the many crossroads decisions.

Mike didn't recover from his addiction before his lawless decisions caught up with him and they ended the marriage. Today he is serving a prison sentence and Courtney is living with a clear conscience, knowing that she made every effort to give him a chance for a new, better life.

The message from this story is to stay consistent with the guidance from your uncommon sense, *especially* when you're at the crossroads daily—when not just one but several critical decisions are cascading through your life. Staying focused on your compelling personal purposes also helps you recognize the wisdom of your uncommon sense as you make the related crossroads decisions.

Can't See the End from the Beginning

Joel and Amy were leading a successful business with all the trappings of that success. They were "party central" in their social circle and living the American dream with all of their toys. They were also successfully navigating the combining of their two families and were enjoying each other.

But in their "quiet times" they realized that they could be even happier. That feeling would persist but could easily be dismissed as unrealistic or unnecessary. Why would they change anything? Instead of dismissing or ignoring the feeling, they started talking with each other about how they might be able to get more out of their life by simplifying it.

Their vision evolved from those conversations. What they realized would bring them the most happiness was to create a new, simple life together. The problem was that neither had done anything even remotely related to the life they were envisioning, but that is where their uncommon sense was leading them in order to enjoy their brand of happiness.

Their compelling personal purposes grew as they started and continued the creation. They wanted to grow their own healthy food. They could make a living from selling that food to the community in which they then lived. This choice would require some land. They liked the idea of owning some secluded land, which led to the idea of living "off the grid" in a self-sustaining system that they created.

Can you imagine the incredulous reactions of friends, family, and others while Joel and Amy started following such a divergent path? They didn't know how they would accomplish each step, but they got started. They couldn't see the end from the beginning of each phase of creation, but they followed their own path, listening to their own internal guidance. They spent years reinventing their circumstances and themselves.

They are now living their modest dream, providing food for their community, working harder than they ever have for less money, and are happier than they have ever been. What they have accomplished is one of life's great love stories—the love of a deliberate life of their own creation, together!

Their compelling personal purpose wasn't the farm they created together; it was the life they created and are still creating. The challenges, successes, and failures are never-ending, but those aren't the source of their happiness. At the end of every day when Joel and Amy collapse in the sanctuary they created for themselves and acknowledge that they are together to face whatever life brings, they are happy.

The message from this story is that you often cannot see the end from the beginning when at the crossroads. Get started and stay aligned with the guidance from your uncommon sense and with your compelling personal purposes.

Learning to Make Crossroads Decisions

As a parent participating in raising five children, I noticed that each child became independent as that child decided to make their own decisions regardless of my input. This transition didn't depend on age or living arrangements. In each case, each child's independence happened before the official age of adulthood and before they left our home and became self-supporting. Since each child was still in the home and not yet "of age," I fell into the trap of thinking I was responsible for their decisions and still had influence. I tried desperately to influence their decisions, which usually meant resorting to buying stuff for them so I would have something to take away when they didn't submit to my input.

My children apparently weren't unique in this declaration of independence. And, like most children, they were not unscathed, but they did fairly well with their decisions. The few disasters were not because they ignored their parents' input on big decisions. Disaster struck when they started the decision process based on their own limited understanding, experience, and reasoning. Or worse, they relied on input from equally inexperienced and limited friends to determine what to do with their lives.

Should they have listened to their parents when making those big decisions? NO!

Well, maybe down the road there is a place for the input of parents, friends, and other people who care. But that place is not at the beginning of the decision-making.

Why didn't I, as a parent, teach them what this book is trying to teach? Fortunately, maybe my bad example is what fuels my oldest daughter, Christie, and her husband, Daniel, to teach this so effectively to their own children. That gives me comfort in not worrying about my screw-ups, knowing that I can always be used as a bad example!

But when parents don't teach kids to follow their uncommon sense, where are people supposed to learn about it and to recognize their compelling personal purposes? Where do they learn to use those tools to clarify the beginning of the decision-making process? And where are we parents supposed to learn this?

The way it works naturally if the parents haven't learned it and don't teach it is that *life* teaches it. Life teaches it through one of two means. We either learn it through the example or mistakes of others, or life beats us into submission through trial and error. That trial-and-error option is an inefficient process.

But now you know to follow your uncommon sense and to establish your compelling personal purposes. If you teach this, then when the people you teach face the crossroads decisions in life, they can have the clarity that others don't enjoy. Teach this!

Confidence in Your Nonsensory Uncommon Sense

We're talking about "voices in our heads" here. Accessing our uncommon sense is not a sensory experience. In fact, Rick's experience of thinking he actually heard a voice is rare. There is no known shortcut to having confidence in accessing your uncommon sense. It comes from developing your awareness throughout your experiences in life.

The more you are consciously accessing your uncommon sense and observing the results, the more confidence you gain in the nonsensory process. In part of this book, you have accomplished at least two exercises in which you recognize the simplicity of accessing your uncommon sense. Unfortunately, simple does not mean easy. Common sense is easier to access when you are faced with simple decisions like which foods to avoid when trying to be healthy than when facing a life-altering decision.

Practice. Record your practice and give yourself feedback. Record the feedback. Whatever works best for you, do it. You might write it, voice record it, or get even more fancy, but "awareness through practice—feedback—record" is your mantra when you want to instill the confidence you will need at the crossroads.

Your challenge is to use your uncommon sense for decisions for thirty days!

CHAPTER 5

LIFE-BALANCE MYSTERY SOLVED BY UNCOMMON SENSE

The two basic commodities of life are time and energy. All people have been allotted a unique quantity of time and energy which they trade for whatever they want from life. Understanding this relationship, people can see that the true cost of a thing is the amount of life required in exchange for it.

—Dr. Richard A. Harper

The question of life balance raises its head when we are doing something for which we had to sacrifice another activity. We're working during a child's ball game or recital. We're out with friends when we could be preparing for an important presentation. We're sleeping in when we could have kept a commitment to get up early to work out. Or we're up early working out when what we really might have needed for our health was the extra sleep or waking up next to a lonely, loving partner. The list of such dilemmas in life is endless. The perplexity is compounded by the preceding quote, or by the often-quoted statement that nobody on their deathbed wished they had spent more time in the office.

So, here is a related exercise for you.

Exercise

Write down the activities that you spend most of your time doing. Then write down your highest priorities, the things you value most.

What are the three daily activities in which you spend a majority of your time?

_____

_____

_____

Now, what are your three highest priorities in life?

_____

_____

_____

For most people, there is a significant disconnect in this exercise. For example, the three most time-consuming daily activities for most people are work or school, sleep, and entertainment or hobbies. But the three highest priorities cited by most people, in no particular order, are God or religion, their family or spouse, and their career (which includes work and school).

When people complete this exercise and see the obvious disparities, it raises a little internal conflict; it doesn't need to. Somewhere we adopted the strange notion that where we spend our time shows what is important to us. The real world, run by natural law, isn't quite that compartmentalized.

Take, for example, sleep. I have conducted this informal, unscientific survey at least dozens of times. Seldom do people ever include sleep as a top-five priority in their life. Yet isn't it always a top-five activity? (The possible exception is parents to a newborn.)

A similar parallel exists in the relationship between where we spend our money and what we value about money. Most people state that what they value most is staying out of debt, saving for retirement or education, and owning a home. Yet those are not the top three expenses of those same people. Real life requires that they pay additional obligations, which sometimes leaves more month remaining at the end of the money.

The same disparities illustrated in this exercise are the disparities that cause so much angst and discouragement when considering life balance. People often feel that they don't spend enough time in the areas of life that truly matter.

Before a solution to this mystery is proposed, it must be stated that misspending our time and our money can be a real thing! And, in the long run, the more we can align our time and money with our priorities, the more successful we will be by our own definition. But the point here is how that should be judged.

My mother was often caught in this trap as she struggled to raise my siblings and me after she and my father divorced, followed two years later by his death. Many of you can relate to the constant feelings of inadequacy as a single parent trying to balance full-time work, scarce resources, bratty kids (my mom's situation, not necessarily yours), and the challenges of life. She seldom felt that she was spending adequate time in any area of her life. In my four-year Little League baseball career, she made it to just one game. Money was too tight for babysitters, so I was often left home alone. However, she was the first example in my life of someone living life deliberately, following her conscience in all of the difficult decisions she faced. She passed away too early to get her children's validation as adults that, from our perspectives, she *always* made the right decisions because she was doing the best she could.

Here is a new definition of life balance for you to consider. And it's a very personalized definition: *Given the current realities of my life, I am doing the best I can!*

What Life Balance Is Not

Life balance happens in the moments of decision during every busy day. Judging your life balance doesn't work when viewed through the lens of only one factor, even when it's the important factor of how much time you spend in each area of life. So many other factors have to be considered when you are making decisions in the moment of what to do with your time. So, life balance isn't only how much time you spend in each area of your life.

Life balance is not limited to sacrificing one activity for a "higher"-priority activity. For example, if I'm at work preparing for an important meeting that was just called, in which a client wants to hear the current status of a project I'm running, and I get a phone call reminding me that I told my daughter I would leave work early to watch her soccer game, what will I do? Certainly, my relationship with my daughter is more important than the relationship with my client, but that doesn't mean that I miss the meeting to watch the soccer game. There are many more factors to consider:

- Is a viable alternative available to make my presentation at the meeting?

- Will the client or my daughter understand if I choose the alternative to being with them?

- How many soccer games have I missed previously? How many are remaining?

- What are the consequences of trying to change the meeting with the client?

- How long will my wife be mad and withhold sex from me for missing the soccer game?

These complex decisions are a constant part of life, are they not? So, life balance is not as simple as sacrificing an activity for a higher priority.

The Key to Success in Balancing Life

The key to success in balancing your life is to follow the guidance of your uncommon sense in every situation. As with all decisions discussed in this book, the sequence here is important. When you face a decision that involves conflicting interests, determine first what the guidance is from your uncommon sense. That is the path to take. Next, allow your head to get involved with that decision you just made by figuring out *how* to do it.

Let's take the example of the dad at work with the soccer game dilemma. Let's say that his uncommon sense guidance is to stay and attend the meeting with his client. His brain is engaged right away, but instead of trying to reason which path would have been the best one, his brain needs to get on task figuring out how to deal with the dynamics at home. Should he call his wife? Should he call his daughter first and explain the situation to her and ask for her understanding?

Or, let's say his guidance is to make it to his daughter's soccer game. The function of his reasoning then is how best to make the arrangements at work. Should he call the client to discuss options? Should he ask his coworker on the project to step in? He doesn't need his brain to reason through the decision, just to weigh in on the "how."

In this situation, his life's priorities are an important factor in how to handle the situation, but they don't dictate what the decision should be.

Since that is an uncommon—maybe even unpopular—concept, let it sink in for a few minutes.

He may or may not be able to explain to his client, boss, daughter, or wife *why* he will do what he will do. That is often an uncomfortable situation. When we are following our uncommon sense, we don't always have an explanation for other people. We are simply doing the best we can.

The Main Blessing of Following Our Uncommon Sense

At the end of the day, when we are reviewing what happened, both the good and the bad, we know we did the best we could. In the quiet times of our life, when we are considering all the choices we have made that brought us to where we are at that time, we know that we are just doing the best we can in each situation, given the realities of our life.

The alternative to using your uncommon sense to make decisions in your life is to use one or a combination of these elements:

- Your limited reasoning and understanding

- Your ego

- Your social mirror

- Your appetites or impulses

- Your fears

Which of those resources is better than your internal guidance system? As a reminder, here are the key aspects of your uncommon sense:

- It is free of fear and emotions.

- It helps you act as your highest self.

- It is completely in tune with the present.

- It is not concerned about the opinions of other people.

- It is connected to the wisdom of the Universe.

Since these decisions, which ultimately compose your life balance, are so completely individualized, the right decision is different for each person and in each situation. Not only can you not rely on others to make your decisions, but you can't even duplicate decisions you have made in the past in similar situations and expect the same results.

Since this life is so complex, isn't it wonderful that life has provided such a resource to specifically deal with these complexities? As you stay aware of that internal guidance, learn to trust it, and learn to expect and accept the natural consequences. This process allows you the comfort of knowing that, given the realities in your life, you are doing the best you can.

An example may help to clarify this concept.

Having lived through being a single mom, then being in the position to give advice to other single moms who had the struggles of life along with deciding to go back to school to earn medical degrees or certifications, Lisa has provided hope with this advice:

> You will probably spend the next few years feeling like you are doing everything half-assed all the time. Allow those feelings, but don't buy into them. You have to judge your efforts by the outcome, not

what is happening in the process. It will have to be enough for you to know that if you were facing the same challenges with more support, more time, and more resources, your grades would be better, you would finish sooner, your kids would see you more at home and at their activities, you would not be sleep deprived, and you would have time for self-care. When you are on the other side of this challenge, you will know it was worth it![6]

While circumstances might be similar, no one else takes the path that you do with the same dynamics. The only valid judge of the decisions you make and the outcomes you produce in your life-balancing efforts is your own conscience. You will feel much better about that judgment when you have been following the guidance of that same judge!

A Different Approach to Life Balance

So, you now probably have been introduced to a different definition of life balance than you had before. You have also been introduced to a different approach to life balance than you have taken in the past. A little further explanation might avoid some misconceptions.

This chapter is not suggesting that you throw out any time/self-management approach that you are using successfully. I have an approach that I have been using since I was introduced to it in

---

6   Lisa, personal conversation with author, October 2016.

the 1980s that continues to make a tremendous impact in my life. This is a quick story about that impact.

When I adopted the self-management process in Rebecca and Roger Merrill's *First Things First* book, as taught by Stephen Covey, the impact was immediate. I began the process one year in the late fall. A few weeks later, just after Christmas, my wife made this statement that startled me: "It was so nice to have you here for Christmas for the first time."

After thinking about that for a moment, I asked, "What are you talking about? I have always been home for Christmas. Even during our time in the military, I never missed a Christmas."

"Well," she responded, "you were here for the Christmas program and to watch the kids open the presents on Christmas Day, but you were never a part of the season. You were always working or had work on your mind."

It only took me a few reflective seconds to grasp her accusation. Her description of my holiday absence was accurate. But this year, the planning process from *First Things First* had me consider my roles in life every week, to include being a husband and father. Then, I would set goals for the week in each of those roles. Apparently, those goals leading up to Christmas included involvement with the family and the preparations to celebrate. To her, I was home with the family for Christmas.

What you read in this chapter about priorities and goals is completely aligned with this approach and with any other approach to time management. Where the impact of following your uncommon sense will make the deciding difference in your life balance is during the "moment of choice."

Priorities and goals are an important part of planning and

implementing your life-balance strategy. When it comes time to live that plan, we all know that stuff happens, like the sudden business meeting conflicting with the soccer game in our example. The authors of *First Things First* explain that you must "exercise integrity in the moment of choice." Exercising integrity does not mean "I made this plan, and nothing will change it!" It means that you make a conscious decision, accessing your conscience or uncommon sense. If you must change your plan, do so by rescheduling or recreating the important event that you will miss.

When you are making conscious decisions about what to do with your time by accessing your uncommon sense, you will know that you are doing the best you can.

Exercise

As you consider your life-balancing efforts, what does your uncommon sense suggest you should start doing in your life?

What should you stop doing?

_____

What should you continue to do?

_____

What should you do better?

_____

CHAPTER 6

UNCOMMON RELATIONSHIP SENSE

To be trusted is a greater compliment than being loved.

—George MacDonald

lying along at three hundred nautical miles per hour at the controls of a military jet with three feet wingtip clearance from another military jet requires that you trust that other pilot with your life. In the military, there were many pilots I would trust with my life, but not with my wife . . . or with my daughter.

As with all other aspects of life, relationships are governed by natural laws. While countless natural laws are involved in relationships, let's consider three of the most foundational:

- Trust, not love, is the foundation of all relationships.

- There are conditions to *all* relationships.

- All relationships have potential conflicts.

The Trust Formula

Trust generally happens subconsciously. But since it is the foundational natural law of all relationships we experience in life, it might be useful for you to have the following formula to use in the event that you need some conscious effort for trusting your life, or even your heart to someone. Trust is situational, and it's individual.

Trusting a skilled pilot with your life happens in a specific situation. Just because that person has earned your trust in that situation does not mean the trust extends to the same person in another situation. You can think of several examples of this. Those are examples of trust being situational.

Some pilots didn't have the same high level of skill in formation flying, so I didn't trust them. Just because you trust one pilot to fly on your wing does not mean you trust them all. Just because you trust the advice of one doctor does not mean you trust all doctors. Just because you trust one law enforcement person does not mean you trust them all. That is a decision about trusting individuals.

Character and competence are often defined as requirements for trust. Let's break that down a little further for purposes of our trust formula. When we are subconsciously deciding to trust someone, we assess their character in a particular situation. Specifically, we want to know that neither their values nor their motives will conflict with ours in the situation.

Be careful with this one. There are not specific values or motives that always apply because only those in this situation are considered. For example, most people will cite honesty as a requirement for trust, because it often is. But can thieving, lying scoundrels trust each other while teaming up to commit crimes? Of course! In their world, there is "honor among thieves." How? Trust is situational. In the situation of a particular criminal conspiracy, the honesty they value doesn't fit the classic definition. And their motives are aligned.

Competence is also tricky as a requirement for trust. We deem someone competent in a situation when they can get us what we want, but it also has to be *the way we want it*. Here is the classic example of that:

Many new grooms get a version of the following advice from a mentor either before or early in their marriage:

"There will be some tasks in the marriage that you don't want to get stuck doing for the rest of your life. Let's use doing the dishes as an example. When your new wife asks you to do the dishes, do them willingly, even smiling as you do . . . and break a couple of her favorites. After a few times, she won't trust you to do the dishes anymore!"

The new bride was getting what she wanted—clean dishes from her new hubby, but not the way she wanted them.

So, to summarize the trust formula, three factors must be present for you to trust another individual in a given situation. That person—

- Cannot have values that conflict with your values

- Cannot have motives that conflict with your motives

- Must be able to provide what you want, the way you want it

Values are what is important to you. Stating that your values can't conflict with the other person's does not mean the values have to be the same. If, for example, you value being on time at work, another person doesn't have to value being on time as long as they are on time while working with you. There is no conflict of values.

Motives are the reasons we do what we do. If one person meets standards at work only to avoid getting in trouble, a person who may meet standards at work to qualify for a promotion can trust working together even though their motives are different. Those motives don't conflict with each other.

Getting what you want from another person isn't enough to trust them. You have to get it the way you want it, like the new bride in the dishes example.

The "smarmy" financial advisor

Here was the explanation a client gave to her financial advisor, describing why she trusted a previous advisor to sell her a certain financial product that turned out to be a good decision:

The client said, "I didn't trust the guy because he was so smarmy."

"Smarmy?" the advisor asked.

"You know, kind of sleazy and sketchy."

The advisor said, "Okay, but you trusted him enough to follow his recommendation for this investment."

The client responded, "Normally I wouldn't trust him enough

to buy a pencil from him off the street. I did this time only because I had done the research, I knew other people with this investment, and he was the only person that could get it for me."

"You didn't worry that he was only selling it to you so he could make the commission?"

"I didn't care who made the commission," the client said. "I just wanted the investment."

Let's consider this scenario against our trust formula. The smarmy advisor's character was definitely in question generally. But in this situation the client didn't sense any values or motives that conflicted with hers related to this transaction. It came down to the reality that he could get her what she wanted. His character was acceptable for this transaction, and he was competent. She wouldn't conduct any other business with him.

You, too, have likely had business experiences in which you surprised yourself, either by trusting someone in a one-time situation that you wouldn't otherwise trust, or by not trusting someone in one situation you might otherwise trust. Consider how those situations fit this model.

In the movie *Ocean's Eleven*, a team of thieves unites to rob a casino owner. In *Ocean's Twelve*, that same casino owner joins the team of thieves to rob a different casino owner, while attempting to double-cross the team of thieves, who know he's trying to double-cross them. How can all of these thieves continue working together? One line in the movie sums it up: "Our interests are temporarily aligned." None of their values conflicted, their motives were temporarily aligned for this situation, and they were all confident they would get what they wanted from the other thieves.

Personal relationships

Your thoughts have probably already turned to more personal relationships: friends, family, spouse. If trust is truly such a foundational natural law of relationships, why do we stay in relationships with people who are not worthy of our trust? Because trust is situational. There is probably not a living human whom you trust in all situations. Test it.

For me, the person I trust the most, in most situations, is my wife. Do I trust her with *any* thought that comes to my mind on *any* subject? No! Why not? For one reason, with my many shortcomings, I am not always able to deliver information to her the way she wants it. (You can fill in whatever subject you choose.) For another, our motives and values are not always aligned on all subjects in all situations (no, not just on sex)!

She doesn't trust me in all social situations either. For example, she will lay down rules for me on the way to parties with certain people.

She might say, "Don't talk with the Engles about politics tonight."

And I ask, "Why not?"

"You know you won't agree," she'll say. "It will be confrontational. Other people will either join in, or it will be uncomfortable, and it will ruin the party for many people."

She's right. She doesn't have to lay down rules in most social situations. She trusts me in most situations, but not with the Engles.

Establishing trust

Perhaps the best use of this trust model for you is for consciously establishing trust with others. In my past sales career, I found this trust model valuable.

While selling financial products on commission as an advisor, establishing trust was critical. Right away my motives were in question because potential clients knew I was going to make a commission if they acted on my recommendations to them. Following this model, I had to do the following:

- Ensure our motives were aligned, meaning that the recommendation had to not only make them more money than I would make, but it would also make them more money than they could make in a recommendation with no commission involved.

- Ensure our values were aligned. They were considering my recommendations because they wanted to follow a plan to reach financial independence according to their definition. I had to make it clear that I wanted the same outcome.

- They had to believe that my recommendations would result in the financial independence they wanted, the way they wanted it. I had to manage our conversation in order to determine not only what they wanted, but also how they wanted it.

Everyone has financial prejudices and opinions thrown at them regularly in the media and in conversation. I had to discover and address the prejudices and opinions of the individuals (both people in a couple) sitting in front of me. That is the only hope I had to align our motives and values and to ensure I could get them what they wanted, the way they wanted it.

CREATE THE LIFE YOU CRAVE

At this point, it might be beneficial for you to pause right now and use this formula for a relationship important to you. Consider how that relationship could benefit or could have benefitted by applying this formula:

- Align motives.

- Align values.

- Get the other person what they want the way they want it.

All Relationships Are Conditional

Since I have put my own marriage up for scrutiny, let's continue using it as one example of applying natural laws to relationships. My wife and I both experienced previous marriages that ended in divorce. So, what was going to be different about this one?

When the dating relationship between Lisa and me started looking like it could work out over the long term, we decided we would deliberately set and adjust all of the conditions in our relationship. It's a continuous effort for life.

Here is how we started: we set the core condition of the relationship. Our core condition is this: if our relationship works the way we want it, the relationship is the most important priority in each of our lives. We wanted to create a new experience in our lives with our relationship at the core.

Your core may be different. Many people will say God is more important, or already existing children are more important, or another commitment is more important. The point is to consciously agree on the core.

With our core established, we then began an exercise that continues to this day. We threw out of our lives all other relationships, values, interests, and habits. All that was left was our relationship. Then, one by one, we decided together what we would bring into the circle of our relationship.

One of the early discussions was about our children. We each had children from prior marriages. Did we want each of them as part of our relationship? Of course! But what did that mean? How would we each interact with each of them? How would we assist each of them in various situations? Would we let them live with us in certain situations? How would we deal with conflicts and keep our relationship core intact? It's a long discussion, and it continues to this day.

Another of the early discussions was about God in our lives. Did we want Him in our lives? Of course! What did that mean? How would we communicate with Him and include Him? How would we align our beliefs and our practices? Would we be religious? What would that mean? What would we do with religious questions or practices that didn't align with our core relationship? That's a long discussion that continues to this day.

And, since sex sells and my publisher wants to sell a lot of copies of this book, I'll share that we discussed the important topic of sex. What role would sex play in our relationship? Whose rules/boundaries would we follow? With whom, if anyone, would we share intimate details? What is safe to discuss? How do we make topics safe that we want to discuss? What is off-limits to discuss? To do? Those are long, mostly enjoyable discussions that continue to this day.

Another early topic we discussed was our friends—each one of them. Did we want this person/couple/family in our relationship?

What did that mean? How would that be healthy in our relationship? As it turns out, some friends in our relationship are only associated with one of us. I want Lisa to continue the rich relationship she has with some of her friends, but I don't feel the need to be involved in most of their interactions. I have some friends with similar conditions involving her. Those are discussions that continue to this day.

What about hobbies, interests, health, recreation? Each of those topics and a myriad of others are important, and we believe it to be important to discuss each one, determine if/how it makes it into the circle of our relationship, then how we need to adjust those conditions anytime the situation changes. Situations change often.

Most of our conversations are rich and about what goes on in our lives every day and about the miracle of our relationship that has remained at the core of each of our lives. The miracles become evident each time significant challenges or conflicts are resolved positively because it's a simple process to weigh them against the standard of how it relates to our relationship.

The point of that example is that anyone, including you, can consciously and deliberately set the conditions in all of your relationships. When you consider most of your relationships, you'll notice that most of the conditions were set unconsciously and not deliberately.

Many times, you will need to do this with the other person, but not always. For example, you can and should decide the conditions to some relationships on your own. You have to decide which relationships are healthy for you and which are not. You have to determine the conditions in unhealthy relationships or to discontinue those relationships.

Conflicts in Relationships

Since conflicts are inevitable when humans are involved, you can also predetermine which natural laws (natural human reactions in this case) are involved and how you can best handle conflicts. For example, when emotions are high, most people's problem-solving abilities are limited. During more rational times, the motives and values can be more easily explored and aligned.

Given those natural laws, your strategy for conflicts might be to allow human reactions in a given conflict, but to not try to resolve the conflict immediately. Your "rules of engagement" might be to get out of the situation, knowing that you will regroup later to work out the conflict.

When you regroup, you can explore the motives and values. That by itself will often resolve the conflict. If not, more negotiating may be necessary to realign motives and values so trust can be reestablished.

For example, I have, on occasion, said stupid things that Lisa has interpreted as offensive. Early in our relationship, she explained why she was diplomatically approaching the subject of how I was handling my relationship with a family member.

"I'm trying to help you preserve the relationship," she said.

"What makes you think I need help to preserve it?" was my terse reply.

We both recognized that our interaction had become confrontational, so we ended that conversation, knowing we would return to it later when the emotions were not quite as tense. We had previously agreed to allow our human reactions in emotional situations and not hold them against each other once we had calmed down to a more rational frame of mind.

The next day, when that time of more rational frame of mind had returned, we revisited the conversation.

"What did you think my motive was for making suggestions to you?" she asked.

"It seemed like an attack, like I couldn't handle my own relationships without help," I replied.

"Do you think that was my motive?"

"No. That was just a reaction during a time when I wasn't sure about what to do. It really wasn't about you."

We continued the interaction, realizing that our motives and how we value our relationship together were still aligned. We established that when we found ourselves in similar situations, we would simply say, "Let's take a time-out from this discussion," and immediately drop it in order to avoid having our apparent disagreement escalate. That would remind us to wait until we were both more rational before we would readdress the topic. We agreed that process would get us both what we wanted, the way we wanted it.

Exercise

I suggest you take the time now to record the results of applying each of the three topics, restated in the following, to at least one relationship in your life. Maybe applying a structure will help. Based on your application of each topic, what will you start doing in the relationship you are considering? What will you stop doing in that relationship? What will you make sure you continue doing in that relationship?

To review, the three topics are—

- The trust formula identifies three components you can use to establish trust with another person.

- All relationships have conditions. Establish those conditions consciously and deliberately.

- There are conflicts in all relationships. Deliberately establish how you will handle those conflicts. Establish that with the other person when appropriate.

My own example of this exercise

Stan works for me as a valued member of the team. I also value my personal relationship with him. I want that relationship to survive the workplace, and even to continue should Stan leave this work for something else. I believe increasing our trust will facilitate that type of relationship.

I'll start discussing with him how we can align our values and motives in relation to him working for me. We need to ensure we both know what the other person wants and the way we want it.

I'll stop making assumptions about what he wants out of the relationship. Up until now I have drawn my own conclusions about what he wants, often being very wrong in my assumptions.

I'll continue encouraging our willingness to re-engage in conversations after disagreeing with each other. We both want to preserve the relationship and are willing to not allow a tense conversation to build barriers between us.

Deliberately establishing conditions in relationships

For this exercise I am going to focus on any unhealthy relationships I might have. I will either establish healthy conditions or end the relationships.

I'll start identifying, with the help of my wife, any potentially "unhealthy" relationships I might have. After defining what an unhealthy relationship is, we'll review any of my relationships that either of us think might be unhealthy. I will decide for each relationship whether to establish healthy conditions or to end it.

I'll stop justifying any unhealthy relationships as defined by the parameters we establish together.

I'll continue this exercise with my wife, discussing each relationship I have from time to time and/or as relationships change.

Deliberately determine how to handle conflicts

Related to applying the trust formula, I will have this discussion and try to deliberately establish how to handle conflicts with Stan, the person who works for me whose relationship I value. We are both a little headstrong and disagree to the point of conflict from time to time.

I'll start discussing with him this idea of establishing ground rules when we reach the point of conflict. I think he might be a little skeptical at first, but will be willing to make the attempt, especially after we have discussed aligning our values and motives.

I'll stop continuing conversations either of us feels have turned into a conflict.

I'll continue returning to discussions after we have extracted ourselves from a conflict.

The three topics of this chapter—trust, conditions, and conflicts in relationships—are not only three of the most foundational aspects of relationships, but they also all have the characteristic that we don't usually establish them deliberately or consciously. We tend to let them occur and evolve as they may. To whatever degree that is true for you, please allow this to be an invitation to consciously follow your uncommon sense as you evaluate and reinforce the important relationships in your life.

CHAPTER 7

UNCOMMON SENSE IN YOUR PUBLIC LIFE

I am not a product of my circumstances.

I am a product of my decisions.

—Stephen R. Covey

When your compelling personal purposes are ignited within you, you realize that you don't have enough time and resources to fulfill them the way you desire. You wish you would have started earlier in your life. You develop a sense of urgency.

The role of your uncommon sense in your public life is to help you recognize natural thieves of your energy and resources. They are hiding in plain sight in our lives. This chapter exposes five of them:

- Do we want to be investing in that which we cannot influence?

- "People join companies, but then leave their boss."

- Subjectivity is the root of all conflict in your public life.

- "Don't expect fish to climb trees." Don't expect the improbable.

- Every purpose needs resources, people, and processes.

As this book is being written during times of political polarization, global pandemic, and historic inflation, the chaos engulfing the globe provides the best reason for following your uncommon sense. It gives you clarity on what to do with your limited time, money, energy, and any other resources. This guidance is invaluable.

No two people have the same path, but your uncommon sense will lead you to spend your public and professional life in activities and situations you can influence, and in pursuit of your compelling personal purposes.

Influence

Think of all the positive things in life each of us could be accomplishing. Does any one of us have enough time and resources to pursue all of those activities that we could influence? If not, then how can any of us justify spending any time or energy pursuing something we cannot influence?

Consider how much time and energy we invest when we have no influence in politics, world events, other people's relationships, and a host of other interests that "steal" our time. For me, it was my time as an avid sports fan. I theoretically knew that I had no influence on the sport, but like every sports fan, I truly believed that I did. I'd rather not confess how much energy I put into helping my teams win. When they lost, that energy occasionally seeped out as a dark mood to those around me. What a waste!

I started my rehab one year when I tried an experiment. When the Super Bowl came around, I didn't watch it. I wanted to see if my team would play the game without me and whether my not watching would affect the outcome.

Guess what the results were? I reclaimed vast amounts of time and energy by limiting myself to watching sports that brought me connections with other people, like three of my sports-fan children. Where did that reclaimed time and energy go? It was almost enough to write a book!

You are the best judge on how you spend your time and energy. If the activity honestly recreates you (the real purpose of "recreation"), then it is a good investment. If it drains you or causes negative emotions or energy, then make some hard decisions. Time and energy spent pursuing your compelling personal purposes are a good place to refocus that reclaimed time.

People Leave Managers, Not Companies

Try to think of a profession that doesn't require you to positively interact with other humans. Even if the primary activity doesn't require it, such as an automobile technician, you still have significant interaction with bosses, coworkers, and customers. Being able to build trust is essential in public and professional life, and particularly with your boss. It's equally important for a boss to build those relationships with the people they supervise.

Many people can relate to Buckingham and Coffman's statement, in their book *First, Break All the Rules*, that "people leave managers, not companies."[7] While the exhaustive research conducted by these authors, including thousands of interviews, supports that statement, the average person doesn't need the proof. He or she already knows, having had the experience or knowing someone else who has had it.

Following is an unfortunate true scenario that could have been avoided. Similar situations are repeated over and over again in the corporate world.

An experienced training director had performed consistently well and had certain expectations about how his annual review would go. He anticipated that his director's new boss would carry on the tradition of the performance appraisal that had been used in each of the preceding six years. In this year's appraisal, the new boss would acknowledge that the new training program the director had designed had resulted in a 55 percent increase in the first-year production of the new advisors, which had already been announced and which had made all of the training team look good . . . okay, AWESOME! He would then bequeath the max annual raise of 10 percent, which the director had earned every year, apologizing that he couldn't award more than that even though the director's work had increased company profits by, literally in this case, millions of dollars. The director would then throw a party for the entire

7   Marcus Buckingham and Curt Coffman, *First, Break All the Rules* (New York: Simon & Schuster, 1999).

department. That would be the now traditional, annual performance-appraisal party.

You can understand why the following actual conversation during the performance appraisal was such a shock to the director.

The boss said, "Because of our problem, I'm only giving you the minimum 3 percent raise."

The astonished training director responded with a long silence as the news sunk in, then asked, "What problem?"

"The problem between you and me," the boss said. "Our poor communication because you resent me."

Still astonished, the training director said, "I'm not aware of this problem."

"Well, sure you are," the boss said. "You resist all of my initiatives and resent me trying to rein you in."

"I didn't know that you were reining me in. Regardless, hasn't my performance been . . . well . . . spectacular?"

The boss responded, "In what way?"

"Well," said the training director, "the new training program increased production of our new advisors by 55 percent. That's millions of additional dollars of revenue for the new advisors and for the company, and a tremendous retention factor for our people."

"That was a team effort."

"That was definitely a team effort, but I recruited and trained the team, designed and developed the new training program, and managed the team's implementation."

The boss said, "Maybe, but that's my team now."

"Of course it's your team. You're the boss! But what I am explaining is that I fulfilled all of my responsibilities and produced incredible results."

"Maybe," said the boss, "but I can't reward you when we are having the problem that we are having."

"What is the problem again?"

Neither person in this scenario had followed their uncommon sense, which could have led them to work on their relationship with each other earlier—before they reached a year-end review. Consider the trust formula, which was not at all in play here: Neither the training director nor his boss had concerned themselves with honestly discovering the other's motives or values. Neither person had considered what the other wanted and the way they wanted it. In short, they let the relationship develop unconsciously, as most people do. In this case, mistrust developed between them.

It's no surprise that the training director from this story left that position shortly after that interaction. Who knows how much more of a contribution he could have given and how much that could have benefitted his boss if they would have explored each other's motives, values, and goals. Alas, they didn't know how to do that. They didn't even realize the value of having those conversations. You now know better! Let your uncommon sense guide you in recognizing these important relationships and putting in the small amount of work it takes to trust each other.

Exercise

In this exercise you will recognize the degree to which your uncommon sense is active in your relationships by identifying its key traits. Those traits of your uncommon sense are—

- It deals with the present.

- It deals with people (including yourself) the way they are, not the way we wish they would be.

- It doesn't get caught up in the emotion of the situation.

Scenario

Consider a recent conflict you had with another person. It could have been at work, at home, or a public encounter. It doesn't have to have turned into an all-out brawl. It might have simply been a disagreement that wasn't quickly resolved.

Consideration 1: Were you open to guidance?

Answer the following questions to yourself to determine how likely it was that your uncommon sense had the opportunity to guide you in the conflict:

- Were you able to keep the conversation on the current topic without bringing up past situations you felt were similar in order to state your case?

- From your own perspective, were you able to explore solutions that would be realistic for both you and the other person to implement being the people you currently were and not having traits, skills, and attitudes that would prevent you from taking the proposed actions?

- Were you able to both reason and communicate without bringing emotion into those conversations?

continued

Consideration 2: Were you able to establish trust?

- Were you able to determine the other person's motives and values for that particular topic, either in the situation or later?

- Were you able to establish what the other person wanted and the way they wanted it?

- Were you then able to communicate your motives, values, and what you wanted the way you wanted it to the other person?

- Were you able to align on the answers to these questions?

Consideration 3: The relationship with the other person

- How would you assess your relationship with the other person since that conflict?

- Were you able to maintain trust in that relationship?

- If not, is it important to you to reestablish the previous level of relationship? Do you know what will accomplish that?

The Root of All Workplace Evil: Subjectivity

Think about the last two or three conflicts you have experienced in the workplace. Let's get to the root of those conflicts. What percentage of those conflicts were caused by subjective work processes?

A subjective work process can lead to disagreements on what was supposed to be accomplished, how it was supposed to be accomplished, how the results would be reported and evaluated, what recognition would result, and so forth. Now, consider the most critical work processes of how you get paid, how you get recognized, how work is distributed, how scheduling is accomplished, how you qualify for promotions, and so forth.

Now, with your experience in mind, what percentage of conflicts in the workplace are the result of subjective work processes or subjective instructions you receive?

I have performed this unscientific and informal survey dozens of times. Without fail, the participants' responses indicate that a range from 60 to 100 percent of the conflicts have their roots here. Then comes the sobering realization from the following question: *Do work processes have to be subjective?*

Of course not! People will always be subjective, but work processes do not have to be. A simple process to convert subjective language or processes into observable actions that anyone can observe requires less than an hour to learn. The work processes are then rendered objective. That system is taught by the human behavioral expert Dr. Robert Mager, in the book he wrote entitled *Goal Analysis*. When you read the book, you will probably accuse Dr. Mager of trying to make money by simply organizing common sense. It's a blinding flash of the obvious. In fact, most methods of following natural law are just that!

Here is an example of applying goal analysis to a critical subjective process in the corporate world:

A financial services company in the Southwest had to have solutions for their sexual harassment accusations and had to have them fast! The company had evolved from its entrepreneurial roots in the 1970s and '80s as a good-ol'-boy culture in which the compliant phrases about sexual harassment had been circulated, but the policies were subjective with plenty of room to protect the leaders who were used to getting around the rules. Now they were facing the harsh consequences of those subjective policies.

Phrases such as "will not be tolerated," "unwelcome conduct," and "an offensive environment" are examples of subjectivity. This is where the people who had caused the trouble were rationalizing their actions and hiding behind the interpretations. The company's approach was no longer working.

The goal-analysis solution begins by identifying all of the subjective language in the policies. Once the subjective language is identified, it must be translated to observable actions. If done in conversation, it sounds something like this:

The boss might say, "There will be no unwelcome conduct!"

The boss's translator then says, "Well said, Boss. When you say 'unwelcome conduct' [or whatever the subjective content is], what actions are you observing?"

"Well," says the boss, "no one should tell jokes that the listeners consider to be inappropriate for the workplace."

The translator responds, "Fair enough. What else?"

"There should be no pictures on display that people consider to be sexually oriented."

"Got it. What else?"

The "what elses" continue until the boss completes the list of observable performances that describe the previously subjective phrase of "unwelcome conduct."

That process is how all of the previously subjective policies and communications dealing with sexual harassment in the financial services company were adjusted. That complemented the leadership's strong message of the cultural "clarification." With the subjectivity translated into observable performances, offenders had no places left to hide.

Calling this a "simple" process does not mean this conversation or the efforts to review and revise work processes to rid them of subjectivity are easy. Much effort is required, but the process is not complex.

The work processes that must be reviewed are all of those that support the message. In our sexual harassment example, processes were in place for—

- Educating people on the subject

- Reporting violations

- Addressing reports of violations

- Taking disciplinary actions

- Reviewing and revising policies

The problem with having subjective work processes is that bosses are in the tenuous position of being the judge. Yes, you want bosses to have good judgment, but you don't want work processes to cause them to interpret subjective guidance on what should be done, how it should be done, and how it should be evaluated. That opens each situation to conflict, which is a tremendous obstacle to performance in the workplace.

When you drill down to the root of most workplace conflict, you will find the disagreement is over a work process that is subjective—left open to interpretation. Even a good boss will find it difficult to effectively defend subjective work processes and systems. Subjective work processes and systems are the dangerous root of most of the evil in the workplace.

As W. Edwards Deming—the acknowledged father of the quality movement—put it, "A bad process will beat a good person every time."

Just like it is in the workplace, most everything that has to happen in day-to-day living is a process of steps that result in getting something done. That can include simple processes such as getting meals prepared, to more complex ones such as living within a budget. Processes can be developed deliberately in which the people involved map out the routine steps to accomplish. But more often, processes develop unconsciously as we go about our hectic day-to-day lives.

And just like in the workplace, the processes in our individual lives don't have to be subjective. All that has to happen is that the people involved must agree on the steps to be taken to produce each outcome, ensure there are no gaps, and make sure the language is free of subjectivity.

Can you imagine a world without most of the current conflicts in your public life? It's difficult. People would have to find something else to fight about!

Exercise

Here is one more example of the goal-analysis process to which many of us can relate:

"Get in there and clean your . . ." The increasingly frustrated parent stopped before the sentence was completed, realizing that his definition of "clean room" and the child's were worlds apart. Resetting, the parent said, "Ben, go in your room. Take all of the clothes off of the floor and put them in the clothes hamper. Take all food items out of your room and put them in the kitchen trash. Empty your trash can. Take all of your toys that are not in your toy chest and put them in the chest. Find both shoes for each pair of shoes and line them up side by side in your closet, then shut your closet door. Straighten the covers on your bed so it looks the same way it does when your mom makes your bed.

"While you work on it, I will write the six things you need to do on the whiteboard in your room. You have just fifteen minutes to do this before I inspect. Do you have any questions?"

The parent translated the unclear work process of "go clean your room" into observable actions and outcomes to define what a "clean room" was.

Don't Expect Fish to Climb Trees

Here is another blinding flash of the obvious that comes from following natural law through your uncommon sense. The phrase comes from one of the beloved quotes by Albert Einstein: "Everybody is a genius. But if you judge a fish by its ability to climb a tree, it will live its whole life believing it is stupid."

What should your public life be dedicated to? People who are not following their conscience—their uncommon sense— to answer that question are, by default, following their limited reasoning, or, worse, their ego, impulses, and appetites. Your uncommon sense leads you to pursue those purposes that will allow you to serve above your base desires and that you are naturally suited for.

The inspiring story of Sir Thomas More of England, which was portrayed in the movie *A Man for All Seasons*, gives us a great related insight to what we should be pursuing in our public life. Sir Thomas was approached by his younger acquaintance, Richard Rich, for a position in court that could launch Richard on a career of power and prestige. Instead, Sir Thomas offered him a position as a teacher. Richard was obviously disappointed.

Sir Thomas said, "A man should go where he would not be tempted. Why not be a teacher? You'd be a fine teacher, perhaps a great one."

Richard asked, "If I was, who would know it?"

Sir Thomas said, "You, your pupils, your friends, God. Not a bad public, that."

Richard sold his soul to someone else, who got him the position he lusted for. He turned on that person and on Sir Thomas and spent a life of treachery conniving his way to the top. Indeed, a man should go where he would not be tempted.

Richard was a fish on a tree—not because he lacked the skill to rise in power and to use it for his benefit but because he lacked the skill to follow his uncommon sense to use his power to benefit others as he followed his conscience.

The question to pose to your own uncommon sense as it relates to your public life is this: Are you following your conscience, or are your pursuits driven by your ego, impulses, appetites, and limited reasoning?

Awareness

Instead of an exercise here in which you use your reasoning, make yourself aware of any guidance from your uncommon sense as you consider this question: *Are you swimming the tree or are you climbing it?* This was a pivotal process in my life when I realized that a major undertaking in my life of starting a business resulted in me trying to swim up the tree. I could see purposes that the effort helped me to fulfill, but I had to move to a pond in which I could use my true gifts, talents, and skills.

Every Purpose Requires Resources, People, and Processes

In addition to the specific skills you need to accomplish your purposes, everyone needs success skills as well. For example, if a person is great at baking pies and decides to open a pie shop, in addition to the pie-making skills, the person will need the skills of raising money to get the business going, marketing, hiring and supervising people, establishing job descriptions and business systems, and the list goes on. Of course, if you have the money/resources, you can buy or hire people to perform these additional skills. Your uncommon sense will lead you to recognize how realistic it is for you to develop or find these skills. If you need to develop them, you can follow the Self-Directed Development process described earlier.

For the purposes of this book, we will explore just three categories of the many success skills required: resources, people, and processes.

Providing your resources

So, what are the resources we need? They can include—

- Money

- People's services

- People's energy

- Equipment or technology

- Physical space or structures

The list can go on. Of course, you realize right away that if you have the money, you can usually rent or buy the rest of the means or resources. If you don't have the money, you need to find other ways to gather those resources, but someone has to have provided the people and money.

Now, this is not a chapter on fundraising. It's a chapter on dealing with the realities of life and on accessing your uncommon sense to assist you.

This concept can best be seen through a filter. Let's use the hedgehog concept from Jim Collins's great insight in his book *Good to Great* as that filter.[8] He applies it to companies, but we will apply it to you. Obtain the book to get the details, but consider these three questions in the meantime:

- What are you deeply passionate about?

- At what can you be the best in the world?

- What drives your economic engine?

That third question will be your filter to identify and provide the money and other resources necessary for you to pursue your passion and the service to mankind that your passion provides. But if your passion and the services it provides will not be worth money to other people, how will *you* provide it?

Well, you may use your "day job" to fund your missions. For example, many of you have the mission of providing for a family. Like most of us, you use a profession to provide the means for that mission.

Your passion may be able to raise its own funds. What a wonderful life when you can align your passion with the same activity that it takes to provide the means for that mission! Professional athletes are one example of this. Many of them get to play a game they love to play while providing for many missions they choose to pursue.

---

8   Jim Collins, "The Hedgehog Concept," Jim Collins.com, accessed June 12, 2022, https://www.jimcollins.com/concepts/the-hedgehog-concept.html.

You may, of course, need to rely on others to provide the means. That is a particularly specialized skill in itself.

We hear the sensational stories of people who have plenty of money but no purpose or mission, who squander the many options the money gives them and end up financially or morally bankrupt.

There are far more stories that we don't hear about: the people with meaningful purposes and missions but who never got to fulfill them because they didn't have the means. They might lack the money, the time, the stage, the energy, or the opportunity.

Missions without the means are just as tragic as means without a mission. In the context of pursuing purposes, money and the pursuit of money are sometimes demonized to the point of making its pursuit an obstacle or an evil thing. Of course, money isn't the goal, but money can allow the goal to be attainable. If your mission happens to be in the overwhelming minority of causes that don't require funding, more power to you! For the rest of us, monetizing is an essential skill set to develop.

Monetizing, simply enough, is arranging for enough means or resources to accomplish your missions. Money is not the entirety of the resources you need, but we are emphasizing money because that is the resource that often is the most challenging to obtain. And even when our motives are pure, we will still need the mighty buck.

We may or may not have the skills to gather the resources ourselves, but if it's our mission we are pursuing, it's our responsibility to gather the resources.

Consider one of the most challenging monetizing efforts that gained world attention. Mother Teresa lived her life helping poor people who had been abandoned. She developed her skills to raise the money. She raised hundreds of millions of dollars to financially support what she accomplished.

- She and her army of five thousand religious sisters lived in poverty themselves.

- She never accepted government assistance and its accompanying limitations and requirements.

- She said, "Poverty is our safeguard," because she did not want to start by serving the poor and gradually slide into serving the rich, as has happened to other religious congregations.

This example isn't intended to instruct you to raise money like Mother Teresa, but to illustrate that your cause, no matter how noble, needs the resources to accomplish it.

Your success depends on the many people involved

Consider the drama of an NFL football star whose story is unfolding as this book is being written. Statistically, he is one of the greatest players at his position of his time. Every team wants skills like his on the field for them. But they can't afford his inability to interact positively with the people in his life. A long list of domestic violence, run-ins with the law, and conflicts with coaches and team members makes him too much of a liability. He currently doesn't have the opportunity to use his primary skills because of the other undeveloped success skills of dealing with people. Other professional athletes with similar deficiencies have had to spend

CREATE THE LIFE YOU CRAVE

time in prison before realizing the importance of the additional skills required to complement their primary athletic skills.

Your success in accomplishing your purposes depends on you being able to build relationships of trust with many people in many circumstances. A conscious effort, guided by your uncommon sense, is required.

Consciously establish processes

Processes are the list of steps you will take to accomplish tasks that need to be done regularly. If you don't consciously determine what processes need to be established and establish them, they will still be created, but through the inefficient and ineffective process of trial and error. You don't have time for that when you are urgently pursuing your compelling personal purposes.

For example, the person who is good at baking pies has opened a pie shop but does not have a regular process for takeout pies. Every time a customer orders, the availability is different, the time it takes to prepare the order is different, and the process to pay is different. Those pies had better be darned spectacular to expect the customers to continue ordering takeout!

Exercise

This exercise is to determine how much of the concept of resources, people, and processes has stayed with you through the reading.

If you were to start your own business right now, what would it be? Have fun with this. You are not establishing a business plan here.

What resources would you need, including the amount of money to start, the monthly/quarterly amount you would need to continue your operations, the equipment/materials you would need, any buildings or real estate you would need, and so on?

What people would you need? Not specific individuals, but what skill sets would be required, to include administrative, marketing, management, fundraising, sales, and so on?

What processes would you need to establish? Include how people will pay you money; how you will deliver your product or service; how you will account for money flows; how you will attract, develop, evaluate, and retain the people you need; how you will market, advertise, and sell your product or service; how you will establish all of these processes and who will keep them up to date; and so on.

Now, back to your uncommon sense and your public life. As a result of this chapter, what do you need to do? What do you need to start doing? What do you need to stop doing? What do you need to continue doing?

CONCLUSION

THIS *IS* THE POWER WITHIN YOU!

How often have you been inspired by the message that the power is within you? It might have been by a speaker, or it may have been written, or it may have been your own self-realization that the power to do whatever you are supposed to do with your life lies within you. Yes, it does!

What is that power that guides you in every aspect of your life, that gives you context for all actions in your life, even the seemingly insignificant decisions you make every day? That is the primary subject of this book—your uncommon sense, your conscience, your internal guidance system.

The skeptic or complete atheist might say that your internal guidance is all you have. Those who believe that nature is the supreme power in the universe might say that this conscience is the spark of divinity that nature provides to all inhabitants of the earth. Those who believe in God might acknowledge it as His spirit that binds all of us together and provides guidance to all those who will follow it.

What matters in this context is not our belief structure but our willingness to draw on guidance that is provided to us with the sole purpose of leading us to be our highest self. This inner guidance is available to everyone. It dictates to no one. We all choose when and if to follow it.

We each acknowledge this inner guidance to ourselves during the aware times in our life when we realize what we *could* be doing with our life. Those possibilities of our highest self are available at *all* times, regardless of age, health, or current situation. Receiving the guidance from our uncommon sense *is* the power within us.

When we are not aware, we are drifting in life.

Napoleon Hill, author of *Think and Grow Rich*, had an interview with the devil, which he chronicled in his book *Outwitting the Devil*. In it, the devil revealed his two most effective principles for leading the "earthbounds" to hell. He claimed the two principles worked on 98 percent of the population.

The two closely related principles deal with habits. The first is enticing people to develop the habit of drifting—to spend their time in pursuits that keep them from their purpose. In the devil's own words from the book:

> My greatest weapon over human beings consists of two secret principles by which I gain control of their minds . . . I establish the habit of drifting. When a person begins to drift on any subject, he is headed straight toward the gates of what you earthbound call hell.

I can best define the word "drift" by saying that people who think for themselves never drift, while those who do little or no thinking for themselves are drifters. A drifter is one who permits himself to be influenced and controlled by circumstances outside of his own mind. . . . A drifter is one who accepts whatever life throws in his way without making a protest or putting up a fight. He doesn't know what he wants from life and spends all of his time getting just that. A drifter has lots of opinions, but they are not his own.[9]

The second principle describes how the devil gets people to drift by using well-meaning, influential people to destroy the habit of people's thinking for themselves, leaving them to live their lives based on the thinking and ideas of others. Again, the devil's words:

Parents, schoolteachers, religious instructors, and many other adults unknowingly serve my purpose by helping me to destroy in children the habit of thinking for themselves. They go about their work in various ways never suspecting what they are doing to the minds of children or the real cause of the children's mistakes.

One of my favorite tricks is to coordinate the efforts of parents and religious instructors so they work together in helping me to destroy the children's

---

9   Napoleon Hill, *Outwitting the Devil* (Shippensburg, PA: Sound Wisdom, 2011).

power to think for themselves. . . . I cause the parents to teach their children to believe as the parents do in connection with religion, politics, marriage, and other important subjects.

Accurate thought is death to me. I cannot exist in the minds of those who think accurately. I do not mind people thinking as long as they think in terms of fear, discouragement, hopelessness, and destructiveness. When they begin to think in constructive terms of faith, courage, hope, and definiteness of purpose, they immediately become allies of my opposition and are therefore lost to me.[10]

The damages caused by these two principles are self-evident, whether or not Napoleon Hill actually spoke with the devil, or even if you don't believe in the devil.

Napoleon Hill recorded this interview in 1938. Due to fear of the controversial content, Hill's wife opposed its publication, as did the next family member who had responsibility for it. It was finally published in 2011.

The book you are now reading is being written in 2020–2022, amid the period of the worldwide coronavirus pandemic and a divisive political climate in an election year in the United States. During this turbulent time, people seem caught up in what they read and hear, and they reflect the perspectives of whatever source they use for their information. The description of people having "lots of opinions, but they are not his own" appears to be accurate.

---

10   Napoleon Hill, *Outwitting the Devil* (Shippensburg, PA: Sound Wisdom, 2011).

Thinking for oneself, which is the natural result of being guided by our internal guidance, does not seem to be common practice. Moving in herds that have been gathered by fear, ego, and limited experience and reasoning seems to be the norm.

If you choose to create the life you crave, to be driven by your compelling personal purposes, and to pursue your own uncommon path through Self-Directed Development, you won't be drifting. Neither will you be allowing others to do your thinking for you. You will be living your life deliberately.

You have a combination of gifts/talents/skills/desires that is unique. Other people may have many similar gifts/talents/skills/ desires, but no one else has exactly the same combination. That means only *you* can accomplish your purposes in life, and accomplishing them naturally becomes your definition of success for your life.

During the aware times of your life, you are aiming at being the highest and best self you can be. That is the person you discovered and connected with through the exercises with your uncommon sense. However, there will still be times when life will distract you, as it does us all, sooner or later.

When distraction hits and you find yourself losing track of where and who you are, focus on what you discovered with your uncommon sense's wisdom.

Here's a useful definition to help you stay connected . . .

**"Remember—to return to an original shape or
form after being deformed or altered."[11]**

---

11 "Remember," The Free Dictionary, accessed June 12, 2022,
    https://medical-dictionary.thefreedictionary.com/remember.

"Remembering" what you discovered about yourself through your uncommon sense is the way to recover from times when life's circumstances get in the way; it lets you reconnect and progress closer to being the highest self you can be—to your life of purpose according to your definition.

Your progress will enable you to use what you've learned, to create your own Self-Directed Development/Self-Development Plan. And that is when the real work begins. That brings to mind this saying: "All grand designs eventually degenerate into work."

Allow yourself to be human with occasional deviations from the centerline of your plan. As the champion boxer Mike Tyson reminds us, "Everyone has a plan till they get punched in the mouth."

Build in your triggers so that when life *does punch* you in the mouth, or you get tired of the work, you can remember to return to your original state and recognize your higher self. Your development advisor can help you with this.

Then, turn to your ever-faithful internal guidance. Your uncommon sense won't send you on a guilt trip for having been temporarily distracted. It won't reprimand or scold you. It won't cause you to be depressed. Since your uncommon sense—your conscience—deals with natural law, it will bring you hope. And, happily, the natural motivator for all of us humans is hope!

Each time your uncommon sense validates one of your compelling personal purposes, you take action with the hope that you can actually be the higher self that you see in yourself. You start caring about that. It's safe to say that you want to be that person because you will be contributing to or helping other people, which gives you further motivation. During the times that you return to the awareness of the person you are becoming, after life has deformed or altered your intended higher self, your uncommon sense will remind you who you want to be. And you will remember that in those times, you must continue listening to your uncommon sense as you evaluate yourself.

Those are the times to relive the exercises you did in this book to recognize guidance from your uncommon sense. If you still need to complete the exercises, do them now. Start recognizing that internal guidance by spending time being consciously aware of it. Continue recognizing the consequences of your choices, and ask yourself if that is what you want out of life—what you *crave* from life. This is living deliberately. It feels good!

As you live deliberately, you notice yourself becoming passionate about actions and activities that help other people. Continuing those activities will lead to your having compelling personal purposes. It feels good!

As you recognize your purposes, you will naturally have the desire to be better at the activities that propel you toward those purposes. You will recognize when you need to increase your skills. As you identify and develop those skills, you will recognize that you are becoming the higher self that you always knew inside you *could* be. You will remember. That feels good!

As you develop those skills, you will recognize the need for more specific skills, especially those skills that will help you be successful in a world where you always need to rely on others for your success. You will have realized the complete journey on which your uncommon sense leads you.

As you become aware of your uncommon sense, it leads you to discover your compelling personal purposes. Then it leads you to align with the natural laws governing the consequences of all your decisions in life so you can fulfill those purposes. Your uncommon sense then leads you to develop the personal skills you need and to develop the relationships that will not only enrich your life, but also be critical for fulfilling your purposes. Our uncommon sense is the power within us.

Creating Your Life through Your Hope

The hope that lies deep within you naturally, past your ego and your impulses and your appetites and your reasoning, is the power within you that creates your life. How?

Hope teams with your conscience, which is in you and in each one of us. Your deepest hopes activate the creational energies of the Universe, which are all present and all powerful. Your conscience, which is that same energy and is with you every day of your life, leads you to your creations. It leads you to the natural laws that govern all of creation—through the maze of creational intentions of all other entities in the Universe—to the path of your life that you create. This path aligns with all others and with the natural laws that govern the outcomes of all decisions and actions. When you align with your path, you recognize it as your creation and as the compelling personal purposes of your life.

No reasoning, science, compliance with a popular belief system, or education are required. All that is necessary is your awareness and for your actions to align with your purposes.

In summary, following are the steps to create the rest of your life's story so every day's experience leads to fulfilling your purposes, your way:

1. Accept the fact that natural laws govern the results of all your decisions.

2. Rejoice in the compelling personal purposes to which you are led every day of the rest of your life.

3. Get used to following your internal guidance system— your conscience—every day, *especially* when you don't want to, because you really do.

4. Embrace the creation of your Self-Directed Development.

5. Master the transitions at the crossroads of your life.

6. Balance your life with your uncommon sense.

7. Thrive in your connections with people, with *everyone*, as if they were the source of your joy.

8. Suck the marrow out of your public life.

9. Create this life you crave with the power that is naturally within you.

Your daily journey begins in your core and projects outward to your major decisions, your actions, your relationships, your daily decisions, and your regular public life. It's the story of you.

ACKNOWLEDGMENTS

The greatest acknowledgment a non-author like me discovers is how many people it takes to drag me through the book-writing process.

For example, I need editors who go far beyond the endless grammar, punctuation, and writing style corrections. Thank you for carrying that burden, Eileen Mager, Nathan True, Pam Nordberg, as well as the entire staff of Greenleaf Book Group.

I need friends and family who are true friends who will take the time to read early versions and provide feedback while attempting to salvage the fragile ego of the fledgling author. Many educated and experienced Conners were involved, to include Lisa, Ned, Kimmie, and Scott. Other kind and helpful family members were Avery Benesch, Tyler Memmott, Terika Newman, and Lucy Lott.

Friends also truly went above and beyond the call, spending their time reading the manuscript and providing valuable feedback . They include Chuck Cotter, Dan Raymond, and Rebecca Pugmire. One in particular was tireless as he met with me regularly throughout the process and provided more than any mere mortal can provide. Thank you for your friendship, insights, challenges, and lifetime of invaluable experience, which you generously shared, Dr. Dick Harper. I'm also grateful to the people who gave me permission to use their stories in the book and the many friends who provided input on passages and the book title.

What about my inspiration? I had to have a muse. This muse had to have powers far greater than mine in order to inspire, correct, be an endless sounding board, and to be a smokin'-hot reason for me to try to show off. Thank God, literally, for the embodiment of His love for me that He provided in my wife, Lisa!

ABOUT THE AUTHOR

Rex Conner has developed expertise in leading people and organizations to achieve predictable positive results by applying natural laws. His professional work has taken him inside more than fifty companies in more than two dozen industries. His background comes through three distinctly different careers with the common element of applying human performance tools and systems as an instructor pilot in the US Air Force, a trainer and advisor in the financial services world, and as a consultant and entrepreneur in the field of human performance.

In numerous keynote speeches, articles, and interviews, people have enjoyed "Train-a-saurus Rex's" new perspectives on timeless principles that exponentially enhance success in human performance.

Rex is a cofounder of the nonprofit Your Uncommon Path Foundation. He is also the cofounder and lead partner of Mager Consortium, which is entrusted to publish and teach all of the world-renowned human performance and training tools and systems developed by Dr. Robert Mager.

His educational background includes an undergraduate degree, two master's degrees, and a doctorate degree. However, his credentials to write this book come more from his awareness of how natural laws govern life and from his sincere desire for you to align with those natural laws as you find what you judge to be the richness that life has to offer you.

Rex is the author of the book *What If Common Sense Was Common Practice in Business?* He lives in Southern Utah with his wife, Lisa. They work hard, play hard, and spend rich time with their children and grandchildren.